JAMES JOHNSTON

1903-1991

To George
with best wishes
Leslie Gilmore

Cover photograph: James Johnston in the title role in the
1950 Sadler's Wells production of *Hugh the Drover*.

Back cover: As Calaf in the Covent Garden production of *Turandot* in 1951.

First published 1994

Farset Press, 71 Kirkliston Park,
Belfast BT5 6ED

Text copyright ©
All rights reserved

Supported by the

ARTS
COUNCIL

ISBN 0 9524842 0 X

Printed by Dundela Printing, Belfast
Cover design by Sketch-It Graphics, Belfast

CONTENTS

CONTENTS

INTRODUCTION

Nineteen ninety-five will mark the 50th anniversary of James Johnston's engagement as principal tenor at Sadler's Wells, and this work is intended as a tribute to the man who has been described as "Ulster's chief cultural export." But James Johnston was never exported: he was merely on loan, and after his 15-year London sojourn he returned to his native Province to pick up where he left off - in his butcher's shop.

Few Ulster artists have made such an indelible mark on British music, and fewer still could boast of such a repertoire. Johnston was as much at home in Covent Garden as Calaf or Radames as he was on the concert platform singing *Ireland, Mother Ireland* or *Ev'ry Valley* from the *Messiah*.

My interest in him was heightened during my efforts over a period of 18 months to overcome copyright and production difficulties to enable a reissue of his recordings on compact disc. Happily, the efforts were successful and a commemorative CD is now available. In seeking support for the venture, I wrote to many of those who knew or worked with him and was impressed by their praise not only for his great art but for his humanity.

James Johnston was a down-to-earth man of the people who rose from humble beginnings to become one of Britain's most popular singers. Throughout his career he rubbed shoulders with all sorts and conditions of men and women, from those in the lower stations in life to people from the pages of "Who's Who", and he treated them all as equals. It was a facet of his personality that frequently got him into trouble because his propensity to speak his mind did not always sit well with authority. Johnston deferred to no one, and no one speaks ill of him for it.

He had 284 performances with the Royal Opera Company, at least 270 with Sadler's Wells - details of many more are missing - and 130 with Dublin Grand Opera Society, always as the starring tenor. To that formidable list can be added many oratorio and concert appearances at every major venue in the British Isles.

Until now, the only reminders of that remarkable career have been a few almost untraceable records that can be played only on obsolete equipment and some press cuttings - for those who care to search for them. The CD and this written account will at least provide some sort of record - albeit limited - for future generations who would otherwise not know him at all.

I am grateful to the following for their invaluable assistance during the preparation of this volume and throughout the quest for the CD:- Mrs Peggy Johnston; Patrick Brennan of Dublin Grand Opera Society; Clare Colvin and Nicholas John, English National Opera; Randall Shannon and Anne Doherty, Opera Northern Ireland; Denis Dowling, George Ferrett, Elizabeth Forbes; Francesca Franchi, Royal Opera House, Covent Garden; Peter Gellhorn, Robin Gregory, Gertrude Grob-Prandl and Charles King; Agnew Hamilton, Derek G. Hanna, the Earl of Harewood; Roy Johnston; Walter Macauley and Leslie McCarrison of the *Belfast Telegraph*; Alice Lindsay of *Opera* magazine; Wilson Logan, Sir Charles Mackerras, Maureen Mahood, Norma Major, Dr Havelock Nelson, James W. Shaw, John B. Steane, Dame Joan Sutherland, Sir John Tooley, and, of course, the many music critics whose appraisals of James Johnston's performances over many years were a rich source of information. ☐

Leslie Gilmore, Belfast, October 1994.

A MOMENTOUS NIGHT

The stage manager eased the heavy curtain aside and peered out into the packed auditorium. Full houses for *Carmen* were not unusual, and certainly not for this new Tyrone Guthrie production which had taken the opera to new heights.

Don José was nearing the end of his act two aria and seemed oblivious to the eyes and ears of his hushed audience. Such was the emotional intensity and clear tone of his voice that he might have been singing the *Flower Song* after a week's rest rather than on top of a punishing schedule that included other operatic and concert performances.

The manager closed the chink in the drapes and nodded to the stage hand who controlled the safety curtain. He had been at the Wells long enough to be able to judge when an audience was about to launch into a standing ovation, and as Don José was on top form, this one promised to be more rousing than most. But then it was often thus with Jimmy Johnston. He had a great - what was it that critic had called it? - an affinity, that was it, a great affinity with his audience, and that frequently led to prolonged applause.

But Jimmy didn't let such things go to his head: he wasn't like some of those uppity singers the management sometimes invited here. He always had a word for the doorkeepers and the stage hands, and sure couldn't they recognise that Ulster accent a mile away?

Just a few bars to go, and the manager nodded to the stage hand to stand by.

"My life, my love, I give to thee -"

How audiences loved Jimmy's emotive phrasing of that line, and the last one-

"Carmen, I love but thee."

The prolonged last tenor note faded away, but the silence in the auditorium remained unbroken during the final few bars by the orchestra. No one wanted to miss a single note of one of the opera's captivating highlights.

There was another couple of seconds of silence and then, as if emerging from a trance, the audience started to applaud, slowly at first and then rising to a crescendo. Some people at the front of the house rose to their feet, and the ovation spread throughout the auditorium and was punctuated by cheers and cries of "Bravo!" and "Encore" from the pit to the stalls and the circle, where the dress suits and evening gowns from a dozen pages of Groves's "Dictionary of Opera" were as vociferous as their less illustrious fellows in the gallery. The general tumult was joined by members of the orchestra, tapping in discreet and measured time on their instruments.

Each time Don José bowed an acknowledgement to the audience and the conductor, the commotion grew louder. The stage manager would have to wait for it to subside so that the opera could continue. He had a timetable to stick to, even if the audience had not. Only one action might stop the applause and allow the show to go on, but he waited a few more moments before motioning to the waiting stage hand.

But as the audience spotted the safety curtain on its way down, the ovation intensified. They had got their money's worth from that aria alone and intended to show their appreciation in customary fashion. The curtain jerked down another couple of ratchets, but to no avail: the audience maintained their lack of composure.

Hang the timetable! The stage manager signalled for the curtain to be lifted. Jimmy deserved his moment of glory: he was the biggest draw the Wells had had in years. The tumult slowly gave way to a buzz of conversation that soon subsided as the audience settled down for the rest of the performance.

The stage manager remained for a few more minutes and then left the wings and went back stage to check on preparations for the following day's performance. He wouldn't be needed to try to calm the audience again that evening because in that cast - indeed, in the company - there were few singers who could rouse an audience in the style of Jimmy Johnston. As he made his way along the corridor that led to his office, he noted that silence reigned once more in the auditorium. □

'A GREAT TENOR'

It would be a sad day for the cultural heritage of these islands if the voice of James Johnston, the Ulster tenor who brought such pleasure to so many, were allowed to fade. Few in the present generation have heard the great voice of oratorio, opera and a host of concert platforms. Perhaps fewer still would even recognise the name, but that is not surprising because more than 30 years have passed since the Belfast butcher retired from opera and exchanged the boards of Covent Garden for his butcher's block in Belfast. He entered retirement with a host of memories from glorious performances and left only a handful of commercial recordings from an amateur and professional career that spanned more than 40 years. Fortunately, some of the recordings that he has left for posterity are classic examples not only of Johnston's great art but of how opera and oratorio should be sung.

James Johnston was principal tenor at Sadler's Wells and Covent Garden for 16 years, from 1945 until 1960, and during that time he sang more than two dozen leading operatic roles opposite such legendary singers as Maria Callas, Dame Joan Sutherland, Victoria de los Angeles, Elisabeth Schwarzkopf, Sylvia Fisher and Dame Joan Hammond. Before going to London, he spent four years with Dublin Operatic Society and Dublin Grand Opera Society, for which he continued to appear as a guest up to and after his retirement from London.

His vast repertoire included fine oratorio in, among other works, the *Messiah, Elijah, The Creation* and Verdi's *Requiem*. He was always in great demand for oratorio, and in 1946 was chosen by Sir Malcolm Sargent in preference to the ruling English tenor of the day, Heddle Nash, for a recording of the *Messiah*. His records sold as well in America as in Britain, and the boxed set of *Messiah* 78s broke all previous sales figures in the United States.

James Johnston appeared on concert platforms all over the British Isles, delighting audiences with his interpretation of songs such as *Catari, Catari, The English Rose* and *My Love's an Arbutus,* as well as with excerpts and arias from his varied oratorio and operatic repertoire. Among his favourite traditional songs were *Ireland, Mother Ireland, The Bonny Labouring Boy* and *The Lark in the Clear Air*. In 1952, audiences at the Henry Wood Promenade concerts voted him one of the two most popular singers of the the season - one of several in which he appeared.

Johnston combined clarity with what the critics called "a ringing Italianate tone", and he certainly had little need for technology to make himself heard. He once read a comment by Sir Thomas Beecham that, "There isn't a British tenor who can be heard beyond the fourth row of the stalls", and filed it in his memory for future use should the opportunity ever present itself. Some time later Sir Thomas was in the audience for a performance of Verdi's *Simone Boccanegra* at Sadler's Wells in which James Johnston had the role of the fiery aristocrat Gabriele Adorno. It was a landmark production because it was the first time that the opera had been staged in Britain, and it is generally acknowledged to be one of the operas for which James Johnston is best remembered.

After the performance the eminent conductor was ushered back stage by Norman Tucker, the chairman of Sadler's Wells, who had translated and adapted the opera. "That was terrific, young Johnston," said Sir Thomas, "a fine performance."

"Thank you, Sir Thomas," said Johnston. "Were you able to hear me?"

"Oh quite distinctly, your diction is good."

"And where were you sitting, Sir Thomas?", Johnston asked innocently.

"I was sitting in the first row of the dress circle."

"In that case it's marvellous that you could hear me because you were supposed to say during a tour of South Africa that there wasn't a tenor in Britain who could be heard beyond the fourth row of the stalls."

According to Johnston, Tucker grabbed Sir Thomas by the arm and quickly led him away before the duel could be further engaged. The Belfast baritone and singing teacher James Shaw, who numbers among his pupils the Ulster singer Bruno Caproni, who is currently the principal baritone with Deutsche Staatsoper, Darmstadt and Frankfurt, worked with James Johnston for many years and knew him well. He recently said of him, "When you asked Jimmy for his opinion, that was precisely what you got - and it wasn't always what you wanted to hear.

Johnston was what the critics called "that rare thing, a lyric dramatic tenor", and it was that quality plus his innate sense of musicianship, his elemental emotional appeal and his ringing tone and intensity - qualities that were also rare among British tenors - that endeared him to audiences. Consistency was also important in those days when singers had to perform three or four times a week, and not always in the same opera.

The Austrian soprano Gertrude Grob-Prandl, who in the 1950s sang Turandot to Johnston's Calaf, which it was said lay excellently for his voice, recalls that one day after a long rehearsal at Covent Garden that lasted until late afternoon and was interrupted only by tea and sandwiches, she said to him, "Now, Jimmy, we can go and put our feet up." According to Mme Grob-Prandl, "Jimmy just smiled and said, 'It's all right for you, but I've got to find a taxi to take me to Sadler's Wells to sing Turiddu in Cavalleria Rusticana.'"

During his sojourn in London, Johnston built up a considerable following throughout his operatic range. He was especially popular in the big Italian roles, which suited him best, and his other speciality was as the country boy in *Hugh the Drover* by Vaughan Williams, a title role which few before or since have filled to such acclaim. In a recent letter, the eminent critic John B. Steane wrote:

"My own memories of him always come to rest on his Hugh the Drover. He was ideal. He cut exactly the right figure on stage, personable but not 'romantic' in any glossy, film-starish way, which would have been quite alien to the opera. There was a bit of cheek about him, a straightforward manliness - and of course all of this would have meant very little if it hadn't gone in company with the ideal voice...JJ had a good strong lyric-dramatic voice, and it was convincingly an open-air voice, and a lover's voice, both of which Hugh's has to be. This of course was in Sadler's Wells, and I'm inclined to agree that he was more at home there than at the Garden. But at the Garden he was a *very* good Radames. We rather took him for granted, but I remember one year in his time when there was an Italian *Tosca* (Tebaldi, Tagliavini, Gobbi) which everybody got very excited about but in the course of which we realised that some of our 'native' singers were at least as powerful as these famous Italians; and in one of the intervals somebody said to me, 'Tagliavini, well, there's style, but I wish he'd sing *out* like Jimmy Johnston.' I didn't quite agree at the time because there was something a bit 'square' (I don't mean in the 'pop' sense), a bit unimaginative, stolid even, in Johnston's singing of Verdi. It was reliable, but I didn't find it exciting - and that was also true of his Manrico, and I'm only sorry to say I missed the *Boccanegra* in which everyone says he was so good."

Experts differed as to which role Johnston could fill to best advantage, but audiences flocked to see him in them all. His favourite role was as Calaf, and although he never sang *Nessun dorma* in a football stadium or in Hyde Park, he sang it to such effect on stage that the audience often started to applaud before he had finished, and after his rendition of *The Flower Song* from *Carmen,* the management frequently had to lower the safety curtain in an effort to stop the standing ovation and allow the opera to continue.

James Johnston was not a tall man and received little formal acting training, but he once said that to him the voice was all - and it was the drama in that plus his technique and commitment and the attributes of a tenor described by Caruso as, "Intelligence, hard work and something in the heart" that enabled him to dominate the stage.

Those who have seen Maria Callas on stage use the word "electric" to describe her performances. Callas combined dynamic acting ability with a superb voice, but Johnston never entirely agreed with what he called the "big-shots" opinion of her as something special. That may have been because she and Johnston did not get on; and that was probably due to their vastly different characters - Johnston the stolid British workman and Callas the International diva. During a rehearsal row he once told her, "Joan Sutherland can sing better than you." It seems that Johnston reserved subtlety for his arias! But their differences during rehearsal or off stage were never allowed to intrude on performances, and in the Coronation season of 1953 Johnston, Callas and Ebe Stignani presented three memorable performances of *Il Trovatore* in Italian. Most critics were dazzled by Callas, but some of them noted that Johnston had held his own in such distinguished company.

Those who remember Johnston on the stage or the concert platform are a dwindling band but, with some reservations, we can rely for an appreciation of his art on the critics of the day. Denis

Dowling, who worked with him in *Hugh the Drover* and who sustained three broken ribs in the fight scene at the hands of Johnston who failed to pull a punch, has his own criticism of the critics. He recently wrote:

> "Reviews by critics in the postwar years were written in many cases with a certain lack of experience of *live* operatic and concert performances, thus I don't think that James Johnston's contribution to the profession was fully appreciated."

Some reviews must have disappointed Johnston, especially those containing comments about his grasp of Italian, but the majority of them were laudatory. After the premiere of *Simone Boccanegra* at Sadler's Wells on 27 October 1948, the *Evening News* critic wrote:

> "It was the noblest singing I have ever heard in this theatre. James Johnston...sang...with a declamatory power and dazzling brilliance of tone that rose to international levels."

As the opera had never before been produced in Britain, a great deal of effort had been put into it by everybody at the Wells. In addition, Johnston was a fine exponent of Verdi's music. One of the reviewers of his operatic debut in the Dublin Operatic Society's production of *Rigoletto* in November 1940 said that he sang Verdi's music as Verdi intended.

Fortunately, Johnston's recordings include the great aria from *Boccanegra*. When it was played by Lord Harewood at a Verdi congress in Chicago in 1974, the Italian experts addressing the gathering demanded to know the name of the "magnificent" tenor and asked whether he could be engaged to sing in Italy. By that time, of course, Johnston had been in retirement for about 15 years.

For a judgment from a perspective different from that of experts and critics it is instructive to look to Johnston's musical peers. It is tempting to suppose that his most fitting epitaph was contained in a terse and telling telegram sent to the BBC by the conductor Sir Adrian Boult. Shortly after the war, Sir Adrian had tuned in to a radio broadcast of *Madame Butterfly* and Johnston's performance as Pinkerton prompted him to send the wire, saying, "At last, a great tenor." That was a striking and no doubt considered judgment by one of the world's most eminent musicians who must have heard many of the great British tenors who had gone before.

The distinguished conductor Sir Charles Mackerras, who worked with Johnston on many Sadler's Wells productions, recently wrote:

> "I was in the Sadler's Wells Opera Company as an oboeist and later a conductor for nearly the whole time in which Jimmy sang at Sadler's Wells. I experienced Tosca for the first time with Jimmy singing Cavaradossi at The King's Theatre, Southsea. I also remember him as Pinkerton and Turiddu in that first season and particularly his marvellous performance as Gabriele Adorno in Simone Boccanegra, his noble bearing and heroic voice in the great aria in Act lll and in the ensemble in the Council Chamber scene are unforgettable. He was in my view one of the greatest of British tenors."

One of the principal reasons for Johnston's popularity with audiences and colleagues in whatever role he played was his attention to detail which derived from thorough preparation. At the start of each opera season he learned or relearned not only the musical scores of productions in which he was scheduled to appear, but those in which, because of a last-minute hitch such as someone missing a train or illness, he might be asked to appear. Thus he featured in many operas with which people do not normally associate him. For example, he was in the second cast for the Benjamin Brittan opera *Gloriana* which was written to celebrate the accession of Queen Elizabeth ll.

Eleventh hour unofficial performances were fairly common in those days, and a role could be carried off successfully - provided it was not a major one. For those, Johnston liked a little more notice, but on one occasion he had just 24 hours to prepare for the leading tenor part in an opera in which he had not appeared for nearly two years. Worse still, it had not been scheduled at Sadler's Wells for that season and he had not revised the score.

At 7 o'clock on the evening of 10 January 1949, Johnston received a telephone call at Sadler's Wells from Patrick Terry, the Covent Garden Opera Company's general manager, who asked him to appear in *La Traviata* the following evening as the principal tenor had fallen ill. Johnston was in Sadler's Wells that day putting the finishing touches to a rehearsal for a performance of *Madame Butterfly* on 12 January, but he knew that he was free on the 11th.

His immediate reaction was to refuse the offer. "I couldn't do it," he told Terry. "I was in that opera two years ago in the Hippodrome in Belfast, but I couldn't possibly bring myself up to performance standard in 24 hours. If you'd like to change the production I could sing La Boheme. I've been rehearsing that for a few weeks."

Johnston was using the tactic that he had deployed nearly 10 years earlier when his refusal to appear in *Faust* for the Dublin Operatic Society had persuaded the company to drop that production in favour of *Rigoletto* in which he made his operatic debut. But Terry ruled substitution out of court.

"We couldn't possibly do that. The house is sold out and we'd have a riot on our hands if we even hinted at changing the programme. Come on, Jimmy, help us out. You can do it, and you won't regret it."

But Johnston was adamant. He had been in Sadler's Wells for just four years and in that short time had built a hard-earned reputation. He knew that as a substitute tenor in a lead role he was bound to attract more than the usual amount of critical attention and that one slip, one error, would be seized upon and could result in damage that would be difficult to repair.

"I'm sorry, Patrick, I can't do it. But as a matter of curiosity, who is your soprano?"

Sensing some interest, because for the role of *Violetta* the Covent Garden general manager had engaged one of the world's greatest sopranos, Terry replied, "Elisabeth Schwarzkopf," and to make the offer even more attractive he added, "and you can name your own fee."

Johnston was still worried about the short notice, but it was an opportunity that he found hard to refuse. A chance to sing opposite Elisabeth Schwarzkopf in Britain's premier opera house was not lightly offered, but to put Terry on the spot he named a fee that was well above the usual rate. To his surprise, Terry said, "That's okay. Will you do it?"

Having stipulated a fee that he felt sure would have been refused, Johnston felt honour bound to accept, and with much trepidation he agreed to go to Covent Garden the next morning for a quick run through the production.

For the rest of that day and well into the small hours of the next Johnston read and re-read the *Traviata* score, and his assiduity paid off because by all accounts after a brief morning rehearsal he turned in a fine performance on the night. He certainly impressed David Webster, the Covent Garden general administrator, because shortly after the performance he received an offer to leave the Wells and join the Garden. He had the distinction of being the first Ulsterman to sing at Covent Garden and, contrary to current belief, that unscheduled performance in *La Traviata* and not his appearance in the premiere of *The Olympians* was his Covent Garden debut.

It must have irked Johnston that he was unable to prepare more thoroughly for that *La Traviata* because according to conductor Peter Gellhorn who directed many of Johnston's performances, including a famous and more than usually tempestuous *Tosca* with the Bulgarian soprano Ljuba Welitsch in the title part, he always liked to be well versed on the role in hand. In a recent letter, Mr Gellhorn wrote,

> "he worked conscientiously and with musical instinct and intelligence...he was always musically exact and had done his homework; I do not remember him ever making a musical mistake in his performances."

Lord Harewood has written that postwar British opera owed Johnston a great deal, and we know the view of Sir Adrian Boult as expressed in his telegram to the BBC. Sir John Tooley, a former general administrator and director general of The Royal Opera House, Covent Garden, who saw Johnston in many performances there and at Sadler's Wells, said of him:

> "He was a magnificent singer with a voice of remarkable quality that had a strong appeal to an audience...Sadler's Wells and Covent Garden were fortunate to have a tenor of this calibre as a company member...his performances of the Italian tenor repertoire made a considerable impact and won him many admirers. There are few Jimmy Johnstons around today and I am sure that most opera house directors would give their right hand to have a tenor like him in their ensembles."

Sir Charles Mackerras, who was present at what he describes as the "epoch making" Tyrone Guthrie production of *Carmen* in 1949 and who later conducted many performances with that cast, said that Johnston,

> "sang and played superbly...opposite the incomparable Anna Pollak as Carmen."

Of Johnston's appearance in *Turandot* the critic of *The Observer* wrote:

> "James Johnston as Calaf sang both beautifully and powerfully; it says much for him that he was not eclipsed by his partner Gertrude Grob-Prandl whose Turandot is truly astonishing."

Mme Grob-Prandl, who was a member of the Vienna State Opera, was one of the most outstanding interpreters of *Turandot* ever to appear at Covent Garden. Her success was all the more remarkable because when she came to London she was at the start of her international career, had to sing the part in English, and was following the great English Turandot, Dame Eva Turner.

Those comments by critics and colleagues raise many interesting issues, but they all display a high regard for Johnston. In view of all the accolades, and in particular the comment by Sir Adrian Boult, why was Johnston not heard abroad, because apart from performances for the forces in Germany at the end of the war when he appeared at the Berlin Opera House and in Dusseldorf in *The Bartered Bride* and in *Aida* with Joan Sutherland and Barbirolli during a tour of Rhodesia in 1953, he did not sing outside the British Isles?

Some 40 or 50 years ago when Johnston was active, the live performance was much more important than the recording. He was required to make only two records a year, hence the paucity of his recordings that remain. But recording in those days was no simple matter: it may well have been more exhausting than a live performance. The voice and accompaniment were recorded on a "wax" and one mistake, even at the end of the session, meant that the whole piece had to be done again.

Johnston's recording of *Faust's All hail thou dwelling* required a high C for him at the climax and a top F above high C for the violin towards the end. Recalling that recording session many years after it took place Johnston said, "I sang it perfectly but the violinist fluffed the top F. I had to sing it three times in all until we got it right."

Joyce Gartside, who appeared with him in many operas, the most notable of which was *Hugh the Drover,* said that her duet with him from *Madame Butterfly,* which was recorded in 1947, had to be repeated six times. She said, "At the end of the recording session we were both exhausted, but the last take was the best."

Nowadays modern technology enables recording engineers to make substitutions from a bank of recordings kept in reserve. Callas once told Johnston that one of her recordings consisted of 21 separate pieces.

In 1958, the year in which Johnston appeared at Covent Garden for the last time, one could see and hear singers such as Callas, Schwarzkopf, Otakar Kraus, de los Angeles and, of course, James Johnston for the equivalent of 50p, and the average cost of a grand tier box was £10. Even in relative terms that was remarkable value, and the live performance was incomparably better than the quality that could be produced from records and the playing equipment of the day, good though they were.

Consequently, in the postwar years singers were kept busy enough in Britain. Johnston's agreement with Sadler's Wells - he always refused written contracts - limited him to 30 appearances a year outside his operatic performances, and he had to turn down scores of concert and radio bookings. There would have been little time for appearances abroad, even if the offers were forthcoming. Unfortunately they were not, but Johnston was not the only British singer who suffered from the policy of opera in English at the time. Dame Joan Sutherland recently wrote:.

> "He sang most of his roles in English as did all of us during the 50s and this was a deterrent to being invited abroad to perform...I am sure his voice would have gained him international acclaim had his career commenced during a later decade."

Sir John Tooley wrote:

> "He was not in the international league although I suspect that was due more to the then prevailing prejudice against British singers than the quality of the voice. My own view is that if he had been 10 or 15 years younger and consequently singing later the story could have been a different one."

The view of Sir Charles Mackerras was that:

> "Although his voice was heroic enough to grace any opera house in the world, I always felt that he was ill at ease at Covent Garden and much more at home at Sadler's Wells. I don't think he felt comfortable singing in foreign languages and the whole production and timbre of his voice revolved around singing French, Italian and Slavonic roles in English translations. He came to professional opera

> singing rather later in life than most people do, but on stage
> he appeared to be the essential macho romantic tenor of
> one's dreams."

The key phrases in those comments are that "He came to professional opera singing rather later in life than most people"; "if he had been 10 or 15 years younger"; and "had his career commenced during a later decade".There is no doubt that his age counted against Johnston and he needed careful make up to portray what Sir Charles Mackerras called "the essential macho romantic tenor".

Johnston was in his 40s when he started his professional career, and in those immediate postwar years budgets were tight, Europe was in ruins, and opera companies must have found it difficult enough to stage home performances, never mind taking a company abroad. But as Dame Joan Sutherland says, the greatest deterrent to being invited abroad seems to have been the policy of opera in English. It gave rise to controversy at the time and had many advocates, one of whom was the late Harold Rosenthal. In *Opera* magazine of November 1955 in an editorial welcoming Mr Rafael Kubelik to the post of musical director at Covent Garden Mr Rosenthal wrote:

> "Mr Kubelik and Opera both believe that as a general rule
> opera should be sung in the language of the audience...I
> know that now the postbag...will be filled with letters from
> those people who cannot stand opera in English at any
> price, who are prepared to go to performances of opera in
> a language of which they do not understand a word, and
> who condemn out of hand all artists with British names, but
> accept most singers with foreign names as being at least
> twice as good as those who belong to Covent Garden's
> permanent company...I would seriously ask those people if
> they expect Covent Garden to produce The Bartered Bride
> in Czech and The Golden Cockerel in Russian."

Through what Peter Gellhorn has described as the "quite remarkable emotional gamut of his voice" James Johnston, by immersing himself totally in the emotion of an aria, could convey to his audience a striking realism. Mr Gellhorn's most telling comment is that Johnston,

> "had a certain innocence that lent charm to his
> performances",

and that view is echoed in many of the reviews of nearly 50 years ago. Of his Manrico it was said:

> "His conception of the foolish boy is a winning one and his moulding of line and phrase was at all times effective."

The success of his country boy role in *Hugh the Drover* was due in large measure to that same candid, unaffected approach.

The drawback of this "lack of artifice" was that Johnston did not always find it easy to be a convincing actor. However, when the artificial scene on stage had an air of reality, he could discard his unwilling suspension of disbelief and act with great fervour. In 1951 when he appeared with Ljuba Welitsch in *Tosca* the Bulgarian singer tried to conceal her failing powers by engaging in histrionics. Every time she came close to Johnston she elbowed him in the ribs or stepped on his toes, and she used her shawl to block his view of the conductor. By deploying such tactics she hoped to knock Johnston out of his stride so that he would make mistakes and draw attention away from her. But her strategy had the opposite effect. The review of the production in *Opera* said that Welitsch's tempestuous behaviour had a wonderful effect on Johnston who sang with greatly enhanced power and "acted with remarkable fervour." The reviewer did not know that during part of the performance Johnston had Miss Welitsch in a half-nelson to prevent her from causing any more mayhem.

During his semi-professional career in Dublin, Johnston appeared on stage about twice a month. He continued with his oratorio and concert work, singing at venues all over Ireland, but his schedule was such that he was able to continue to manage his butcher's shops in Belfast or to ensure their efficient running when he was not there. All that changed when he moved to Sadler's Wells towards the end of the war.

When he became a full-time professional singer the pressures became much greater. He went from two performances a month to three or more a week, and although for those days he was reasonably well paid, his salary was not large enough to have enabled him to survive if he had had to retire early of if for any reason he did not feel suited to the professional scene and wanted to return to Belfast. Moreover, the milieu in which he found himself was full of uncertainty.

For those reasons not only did he retain his Crumlin Road butcher's shop but bought two more on the Lisburn Road and Sandy Row in Belfast. He said from the start that he wanted to retire gracefully when he was at the top - and that was where he remained until, in the words of the great English soprano Isobel Baillie with whom Johnston made the recordings of the *Messiah* and *Elijah,*

> "he returned to his native Belfast, disappearing as abruptly as he had first appeared."

Johnston once told a friend, "The pace was hectic in those days. I saw many singers who felt that the pace was becoming too much for them being passed over for roles. Then when it was felt that they could not fill even small roles, they were unceremoniously dumped. I vowed that that would never happen to me."

Perhaps Johnston owed more to his business interests in Belfast than he realised. They were a fall-back, an insurance against a change of management or policy or some accident of fate that might render him unable to sing, and they allowed him to pursue his singing career unhindered by any worries about how he would survive when he eventually had to retire. There were no nagging doubts at the back of his mind about pleasing the critics or his paymasters, and he was free to interpret his roles as he saw them. That he did so with such great success is a tribute to what Mr Gellhorn called his "musical instinct and intelligence."

James Johnston was a natural singer. As one critic put it, "There was nothing confected about the voice: it just flowed out." His confidence in his own ability and the ease with which the voice was produced, enabled the critic Cecil Smith to write in *Opera* magazine in November 1955 of Johnston's singing of Cania that,

> "his elemental emotional appeal and confident delivery made theatrical pygmies of everyone else on stage, and even made the chorus and orchestra seem half-hearted."

Mr Smith said that the opera was "overproduced" and that the producer,

> "needs to realise that one singer with Mr Johnston's propulsive force is ten times more interesting and exciting than all the fussy business a stage director can dream up."

Another of Johnston's attributes for which he owed much to his early days in the butcher's shop was his stamina. In a busy week at Covent Garden he could be scheduled to sing the lead in four or five performances of perhaps different operas, and may have had to make last-minute unscheduled appearances. Rehearsals for current and forthcoming productions had to be fitted in, plus a concert or two in the provinces and perhaps a *Messiah, Elijah,* or *Creation* at the Royal Albert Hall or a radio broadcast.

It mattered not to audiences at a Saturday performance at Sadler's Wells or Covent Garden that the cast had already staged many other performances that week. They wanted fresh, high-quality performances with no hint of staleness or shallowness of tone, and it is a great tribute to the hard-worked artists of those days that top quality performances were invariably what audiences got.

His early days in the butcher's shop in demanding physical activity gave him the stamina to stay the course in his singing career, and that vigour stayed with him throughout his life. When Johnston was in his 80s he was interviewed for a series of radio programmes. The interview session for each programme lasted for about two and a half hours and the recording was subsequently edited for transmission. At the end of each session all those involved, including the interviewer, the producer and the sound engineers were almost exhausted, but Johnston was sitting upright in his seat, in the words of the interviewer, "as fresh as a daisy and ready for more."

James Shaw, a singing companion of Johnston's in the 1940s, relates a similar story which shows that even in old age Johnston had lost little of his power. In retirement he often visited his old friend and dropped in one day accompanied by a singer who had approached him for an appraisal because he had been told that he "sounded like James Johnston." Mr Shaw agreed to hear the singer, and accompanied him on a rendition of *Ev'ry Valley* from the *Messiah.*

Johnston, the man of countless oratorio performances, parked himself on the settee, listened attentively for a few minutes and then started to fidget. Finally, he could contain himself no longer. "No, no, young man," he said, pulling himself up from his seat, "you need more exultation in the voice. Try it like this." And to the accompaniment of Mr Shaw, he launched into what must have been one of his last renderings of *Ev'ry Valley.*

"We didn't go right to the end of it because that would have been too much for him," said Mr Shaw. "But he was in his 80s and the phrasing and the tone of the voice were almost as good as they had been 30 or 40 years before. I said to him, 'Jim, if you had just kept practising you could still be singing.'"

James Johnston died on 17 October 1991 at the age of 88. Just three weeks before his death he was in the audience at the Grand Opera House in Belfast.   □

The Cedar Quartet in which the young James Johnston joined brother-in-law Billy Carson (right). Also in the photograph are the two other members of the group, Rita Liggett and Evelyn Gibb.

The Duke in Rigoletto *was the role in which James Johnston made his operatic debut in the 1940 production by Dublin Operatic Society. He moved shortly afterwards to Dublin Grand Opera Society for which he had some 130 performances.*

'YOU'RE NOT A BARITONE'

James Johnston was born on 11 August 1903 at 92 York Road, Belfast, where his father owned a butcher's shop. There has been some uncertainty about his date of birth - Groves states "c. 1900" - but his birth certificate clearly shows 1903, and there is no reason to dispute that. However, for some reason best known to himself, he always celebrated his birthday on 13 August. Some tenors in romantic leading roles used to pretend that they were younger than they were, but Johnston always looked much younger than his years. He had a fresh complexion and a full head of hair, and when his fans assumed that he was a certain age which did not accord with reality, he saw no reason to dissuade them. As Sir Charles Mackerras says, he was far older than he admitted to.

He was the third of seven children born to Samuel and Edith Johnston, their first child being Sarah whose husband was instrumental in introducing the young James to music, for there was no musical history in the family. Their second child was Dolly, and then James was born followed by William, Isobel, Sidney and Norman, who in later years joined his brother James in an expanded family business.

Together with his brothers and sisters, James attended Duncairn Gardens Methodist Church School. While James was still a schoolboy, Sarah married a successful amateur baritone, Billy Carson, who sang in a quartet and entered numerous solo competitions. Brother-in-law Billy used to practice at home and was followed around by the young James, who mimicked his singing and found that his vocal range was at least as extensive. At the age of 14 he decided to enter a competition for which Billy was the favourite, and to his surprise he beat his brother-in-law and won.

That was the first of many competitions which the teenage Johnston entered, and he was placed first in all of them - always as a baritone. At the age of 14, he was in Jennymount Methodist church choir, of which he was a member for four years, and during that sojourn he joined his brother-in-law's mixed quartet. In those days during and after the first world war, there was great scope for such ensembles. Radio was in its infancy, few people could afford receivers, and a local broadcasting station was still

21

some years away. When one was eventually established in the mid 1920s, it provided even more scope for local artists.

One of the main forms of entertainment was the concert in the local church or village hall and, additionally, there were far more music competitions and *feis* than there are today. Quartets, trios, soloists, choirs and instrumentalists played to packed houses and their efforts received extensive coverage in the press. There was ample scope for the teenage Johnston to enjoy himself as a baritone and to sweep the boards in competitions all over Ireland.

In the years before the second world war, Northern Ireland had many mixed and male voice choirs, each of which held an annual concert. The venues were the Ulster Hall and the Assembly Hall in Belfast, which could accommodate an audience of about 2,000. For those weekly Saturday night choral concerts, which continued right up until the mid 1950s when television began to have an impact, every seat was filled.

The concerts started at 7.30 and the audience did not feel that they had got their money's worth if the entertainment did not continue for at least four hours. The season lasted from about September until the following spring, and in addition to the choral works, the concerts included solos, duets, trios and quartets. But the bill was one of great variety and also contained instrumentalists, comedians, story tellers - all the ingredients of the traditional Ulster entertainment. It was at these that James Johnston gained much of his concert platform experience, as did many other fine Irish musicians and singers, such as baritones Hooton Mitchell and James Shaw, both of whom appeared with Johnston in many performances of the *Messiah* and *Elijah,* and the bass Billy Broderick, who died in his late 30s.

Johnston continued to appear at the Belfast concerts in the 1940s and 1950s when he was established in London, travelling back to Belfast about once a month. He often brought with him some of his colleagues from Sadler's Wells and Covent Garden, and they and Johnston appeared not only at the Belfast venues, but in halls throughout the Province.

Another of the regulars was the baritone George Beggs, whose singing of Percy French songs has never been surpassed. His pursuit of singing followed a similar line to that of Johnston, although in reverse: he started as a tenor and developed into a baritone. He was signed up by Columbia to record a number of his most popular songs, but a short time before he was to leave for the recording studios in London he suffered a heart attack, which he blamed on his singing.

Although he recovered and lived for many years, he refused to sing again and no commercial recordings were ever made.

Johnston's first professional engagement was at the wedding in Cushendall Methodist church of the sister of Jack Sayers, who was then the editor of the *Belfast Telegraph*. He was paid 10/6, about 50p, for his efforts, but he didn't feel right about accepting money for singing in church, and when he talked it over with his parents it was decided to pay back the fee. That puritan attitude on the part of Johnston's father was later to deny him a chance to study music abroad.

At the age of 18, Johnston was directed for an assessment of his voice to Bertie Scott, who had been a pupil of Plunkett Green, probably the most distinguished singing teacher of his day. Green, who was born in Wicklow in 1865, studied in Germany, Italy and London and his repertoire included opera, oratorio and recitals. Some songs were specially written for him by, among other composers, Stanford and Parry. In the 1920s Scott was living and working in London as a singing teacher, but he visited Belfast occasionally to hear and advise promising singers. Johnston was ushered into Scott's presence and promptly launched into a couple of verses of, "When you're jog, jog, jogging along the highway". Scott's verdict was that Johnston had "a good, natural voice" and he added, "But you're a bit young. Come back and see me again in about three years." But the appointment was not kept and some 15 years were to pass before Johnston came into contact with Scott again.

One of Northern Ireland's most prestigeous music festivals has always been the one held in Ballymena, and a competition there in 1924 marked a turning point for Johnston. As usual, he had entered as a baritone and sang with his customary clarity. Even in those early days he had a great affinity with audiences, and the applause for Johnston seemed to point to yet another victory. But the adjudicator, E. T. Davies of Bangor, had other ideas. In the summation that preceded the awards he told the audience, "You think you know who has won the baritone prize, but you are wrong because James Johnston, the lad who gained the greatest applause, is not a baritone, he's a tenor.

I hope that if his people do not have the means to send him to Italy or even to me in Bangor, that somebody in the audience will be big-hearted enough to put up the money."

Johnston, who was present in the hall, remarked to a colleague, "That old boy is doting. I'm no tenor." Later that day on his way out of the building he encountered the adjudicator in a corridor and promptly tackled him about the result of the competition, the first one that he had ever lost. Johnston told Davies, "You said in there that I'm a tenor, but that's not right. I've been singing for years as a baritone, and that's what I am."

But Davies was not persuaded.

"My judgment is right," he said. "You are a tenor, and if you will come to me in Bangor for lessons I will make you a good tenor."

Johnston politely declined the offer but the next morning while he was working in his father's shop, a member of the audience in Ballymena arrived and made him an offer which, if it had been accepted, would have put Johnston on the road to a much earlier start in opera.

"Have you thought about what the adjudicator said?" asked Johnston's visitor.

"That old boy was talking nonsense. I'm not a tenor and I don't want to be one."

"I think he was right," said his prospective benefactor, who was the uncle of a local tenor, James Patterson, "and I'm willing to pay to send you to Italy for two years so that your voice can be properly trained."

It was an offer that Johnston found hard to resist. His competition prospects had just taken a nosedive because how could he continue to sing as a baritone when a respected adjudicator whose view would soon be widely circulated had judged him to be something else? But the young Johnston, then approaching the age of 21, was unwilling to accept the offer without his father's consent, and he asked his visitor to return to the shop the following day when his father would be there.

Next morning both father and son were working in the shop when the man who had made an offer that most young singers and their parents would have accepted without question, returned to York Road and repeated his proposal. But Johnston senior was far from impressed.

"No son of mine is going on the stage," he told his affluent visitor, "it's the sure way to hell!" He could not be persuaded to give his permission and said that if James decided to ignore his wishes and go anyway, he would receive no extra financial help from the family. He refused to listen to further entreaties and the discussion ended acrimoniously when Johnston senior forcibly ejected his well-meaning visitor from the shop.

James must have been bitterly disappointed at the outcome, and such an opportunity did not come his way again. Some 17 years were to pass before he was given the chance to enter the world of opera. He must have reflected often on that missed opportunity. A few years before his death he was asked whether he had any regrets about his career and he replied, "None, but I'm sorry that it wasn't longer. If my father had allowed me to go to Italy when I was about 20 I could have maintained better connections, but I didn't do too badly."

Following the shop debacle, Johnston continued to sing in his mixed quartet and in competitions and *feis,* although by now he had taken the advice of the Ballymena adjudicator and was singing as a tenor. He was now in business on his own, because in his mid 20s he opened a butcher's shop at 12 York Road and later bought two more in Belfast, at 66 Sandy Row and 112 Lisburn Road. In the 1930s he was engaged as the paid tenor in St. Anne's Church of Ireland Cathedral in Belfast, in line with the policy of having one paid singer in each voice.

In the 1930s, by far the best male quartet in the Province was the Mayfair Glee Singers, which was managed by Bertie Scott, the singing teacher who had told Johnston to see him again in three years. The first tenor in the quartet was Albert Clarke, the second was Fred Mackie and the bass singers were brothers Tom and Davie McAlpine, both of whom were pupils of Bertie Scott and sons of the blind Ulster singing teacher Jack McAlpine. In 1937, within weeks of a scheduled radio broadcast by the group, Fred Mackie was killed in a motor-cycle accident at Cromkill near Ballymena, which meant that for the broadcast the quartet had no second tenor.

One of the McAlpine brothers suggested to his father an approach to "that young fellow Johnston in the cathedral choir." Johnston was invited to join the quartet for the broadcast and was told, as happened often during his later career, that there would be little time for practice for the broadcast. But he was never one to shirk a singing challenge and the vacancy was filled. He was not a great sight reader, but he had a prodigeous memory and was ready for the broadcast in time. It was such a success that he became a permanent member of the quartet.

During their concert appearances all over Ireland, the Mayfair Glee Singers had numerous solo spots, and Johnston quickly became the group's tenor soloist. It was those performances which brought him to the attention of Godfrey Brown, a friend of Sir Edward Elgar and conductor of Belfast Philharmonic Society, and Johnston was invited to sing the tenor part in the society's frequent productions of the *Messiah* and *Elijah*. The regular baritone was the fine Ulster singer Hooton Mitchell. With the outbreak of war, Belfast Philharmonic found it impossible to recruit guest artists from the mainland, and Johnston became a permanent feature of the society's oratorio productions. But he continued to appear with the Mayfair Glee Singers and to sing in the cathedral choir and made frequent solo concert appearances and broadcasts on local radio.

Not far from St. Anne's cathedral there are two other Belfast churches - Rosemary Street Non-Subscribing Presbyterian and St. Mary's Roman Catholic in Chapel Lane - and Johnston sang in the the premises of all three. Rosemary Street recently celebrated its 350th anniversary and was the first church to be built in Belfast on the banks of the Farset, which now runs under High Street in a huge culvert. The church was built for the worship of Scottish Covenanter settlers; and St. Anne's, which was for settled English Anglicans, and St. Mary's were constructed soon afterwards. The congregations of all three churches have always maintained close relations.

Johnston frequently turned up for Sunday evening service in St. Anne's wearing a dinner suit under his cassock. At the end of the service he would leave the cassock in the vestry and hurry across to St. Mary's church hall to take part in a charity concert organised by the Young Philanthrophists. In so doing he was well ahead of his time because in those days Sunday activities that contained even a hint of entertainment were frowned upon. Johnston senior would not have approved of his son's engagements, charity or no charity.

Some idea of Johnston's confidence in his own ability may be gained from two occurrences during the early 1940s. Just before a performance of the *Messiah* in Ballymena in December

1941, Hooton Mitchell fell ill and Belfast Philharmonic had no replacement. Johnston suggested that James Shaw, then aged 17, should be engaged. Mr Shaw agreed, and sang with Johnston in many subsequent oratorio performances. On one occasion they were booked for a performance of the *Messiah* at Northern Ireland's premier venue, the Ulster Hall, and the teenage Shaw viewed the large audience with great trepidation. With typical frankness Johnston asked, "What are you nervous about, boy?"

"All these people - look at the size of the audience. I've never had to sing in front of such a large crowd."

But Johnston was quite nonplussed. "You're being paid for this performance, aren't you?"

"Yes," said Shaw.

"Well, you can be quite sure that if anybody in that audience could sing the part better than you he would have been engaged to do it."

Johnston once phoned James Shaw on a Thursday and asked, "Do you know the trio from Faust?"

"No, I don't".

"Well, you had better learn it because you're singing it with me on Saturday night in the Ulster Hall."

Mr Shaw later recalled that he "sweated blood" so that he would be ready in time - and he was.

On another occasion the two were engaged to sing at a Belfast dinner and at the end of the evening the treasurer of the society running the function asked, "How much do I owe you?"

"That will be 15 guineas," said Johnston, "10 guineas for me and five guineas for the lad because he's just learning the business."

"What!", said the treasurer, "£15.15! That's ridiculous. You were working for only half an hour. How do you arrive at that figure?"

"Well," said Johnston, "the fee is 15 shillings for the time and £15 for knowing how to use it."

The full amount was paid without further ado.

In the mid 1930s and probably on the advice of Godfrey Brown of Belfast Philharmonic Society, Johnston became a pupil of John Vine, the organist and choirmaster of St. Judes's Parish church on Belfast's Ormeau Road.

Before that, Johnston did not have a singing teacher and was largely self-taught: which supports the view of Leslie

McCarrison, music correspondent of the *Belfast Telegraph,* that "Johnston was a natural singer in every sense of the term."

John Vine was a native of Durham and came to Northern Ireland in 1919 to take over as organist in the parish church in Hillsborough, County Down on the death of the resident organist, William Harty, the father of Sir Hamilton Harty. He moved to St. Jude's in 1921 and remained there until his death in 1953. Among his pupils was the Northern Ireland contralto Heather Harper.

Vine was an accomplished and many-talented musician. He first came to prominence on Tyneside as a conductor of brass bands and took tenor lessons from Dr. Whittaker, later professor of music at Glasgow university, and became the tenor soloist in Whittaker's acclaimed Bach choir. Shortly after he moved to Northern Ireland he mentioned to Godfrey Brown that he could play every brass instrument, and was told by Brown, "If you had lived in Northern Ireland you would be able to play the big drum as well."

James Johnston owed much of his individual style of singing and his flair for interpreting a composer to John Vine's tuition because Vine's primary concern was the development of a pupil's individual skill applied to the interpretation of the composer's intention and he never sought to tinker with a natural voice. He once told a pupil who had just finished a Mozart song, "You sang that well."

"Yes," said the pupil, "I think so."

"And you know it well," said Vine, "but not as Mozart knew it."

Vine was also renowned for his arrangements of Irish folk songs, many of which are still in use throughout the world. At the Command performance in the Royal Albert Hall to celebrate the accession of George Vl, his arrangement of *The Oul Lammas Fair at Ballycastle,* which was sung by the Ulster contingent, was the most popular item in the concert. He had a profound influence not only on James Johnston but on the musical life of the Province. It was John Vine and Godfrey Brown who impressed on Johnston the importance of clear enunciation. Vine told him, "When you sing nobody should be able to tell where you come from."

Both men told Johnston to work on getting rid of the Irish pronunciation of the "e" vowel, which gives some Irish tenors a reedy sound. That problem was quite easy to solve because Johnston's early days as a baritone stood him in good stead when he became a tenor. The rich, baritone/tenor sound gave him an Italianate ring and not the anaemic, reedy sound of so many British tenors of the time. It was probably that quality that led Sir Adrian Boult to pen his telegram to the BBC. Vine succeeded admirably in inculcating in his pupil an adherence to clear prounciation. It would have been interesting to sit in on some of the Tynesider's elocution lessons with his Belfast-Ulster pupil.

People were occasionally referred for assessment to John Vine by other singing teachers, but on one occasion a young policeman from Londonderry contacted him personally and asked for some help. The lesson had to be fitted in between other appointments and overran into Johnston's time.

The pupil was Joseph McLoughlin, but when he later turned professional he adopted the name of Josef Locke. Johnston, who held Locke in high regard, was not to meet him again until many years later when the ex-policeman was attracting large crowds to Blackpool pier. By then, Johnston was in Covent Garden, but Locke invited him to join his Blackpool troupe. It was an attractive offer, but Johnston turned it down. He was a classical musician and probably felt that the showbiz atmosphere of Blackpool would not have been to his taste.

In December 1939 on the strength of his singing in a performance of the *Messiah* in Londonderry, Johnston was invited to appear in a production of *Merrie England,* which was scheduled for the following year in that city. He had not appeared in opera or operetta but was willing to give it a try and agreed to do it.

In the audience on opening night was Colonel Bill O'Kelly of the Irish Army who within a year was to play a leading part in founding Dublin Grand Opera Society. At that time he was looking for a tenor for the lead part in a forthcoming production of *Faust* by Dublin Operatic Society.

O'Kelly was not merely a first-class administrator and a driving force in efforts to expand the musical life of Dublin, but a fine baritone with an ear for a good singer. After hearing Johnston he formed the judgment that the Belfast man would be admirable in that opera, and that judgment was subsequently borne out because just a few years later it was said that a night with Johnston in the title role in *Faust* "would sell out Sadler's Wells fast."

O'Kelly approached Johnston after the Derry performance and asked whether he would be interested in the part in the Dublin production.

"It's not a case of whether I'm interested," said Johnston. "I'm not an opera singer, I'm an oratorio singer and I don't know anything about opera."

"Oh," said the colonel, "and what was that you have just been singing?"

"That was just a musical play," said Johnston. "I wouldn't be up to singing opera."

Because of the war, which by then had entered its second year, O'Kelly was finding it increasingly difficult to import singers, and he was not about to take no for an answer when he had found a good local one. He later wrote to Johnston, again offering the title part in *Faust*. Johnston was reluctant to lose such an opportunity, but he knew little about the work, so he immediately went to Vine for advice.

Vine's first question was about the timing, and when Johnston told him that the opera was to open in six weeks, his reaction was immediate.

"That's far too short a time, and anyway you're not ready for Faust", he told his pupil, and to prove the point he played Johnston a recording of the *Faust* cavatina *All hail thou dwelling*. But he cautioned against precipitate action.

"Don't turn them down flat: you want to leave your options open for the future. What operas do you know?"

"I have heard a few," said Johnston, "but the only one I've seen on stage is Rigoletto."

"Right," said Vine, "send O'Kelly a wire and say that if it had been Rigoletto or something like it you would have considered it. That should keep you right for future offers."

Johnston accepted the advice and sent a telegram at once. To his surprise back came an immediate reply, "Rigoletto it is. You will sing the Duke of Mantua and you have six weeks to learn it." Colonel O'Kelly had persuaded the company to change the opera, and Johnston felt honour bound to accept the role being offered.

Once again he consulted his mentor on the Ormeau Road. When Vine came to the door, without a word Johnston handed him the telegram from Dublin and waited for his reaction. Vine read it slowly, handed it back to Johnston, and then started to laugh.

"You'll n-never d-do it," he said. Vine had a speech impediment which tended to get worse when he was agitated or excited. "Six weeks is f-far too short a time."

"You got me into this," said Johnston, "and you'll have to get me out of it."

Vine beckoned him into the house and the two men went to the study.

"What do you mean by out?", said Vine. "Are you interested in doing it: do you want to do it?"

"It's a great opportunity and I intend to take it," said Johnston. "Will you take me through it?"

"Of course, but you'll need to come to me every day for the next six weeks - and I still don't think that's enough time."

But Johnston was determined to make a success of his first big operatic appearance, and for the next six weeks he and Vine worked assiduously on the *Rigoletto* score. To Vine's surprise, Johnston mastered it, and on 30 November 1940 he made his operatic debut in the Gaiety Theatre, Dublin. The cast included May Devitt, Geraldine Costigan, John Lynskey and Jack Harte, and in one respect Johnston must have felt quite at home because the orchestra was conducted by Godfrey Brown of Belfast Philharmonic. Of that performance the *Irish Times* critic wrote:

"Much interest was taken in the appearance of James Johnston as the Duke of Mantua. Familiar to many for his work in Oratorio and on the concert platform, he was making his first appearance in grand opera, and certainly he has every reason to be satisfied with his debut. He has a voice of lovely lyrical quality and he sang with the ease of the perfect technician. 'La Donna e Mobile' and 'Questa Quella' were beautifully sung - the only criticism possible being that they had just the faintest suggestion of the concert hall. A little more gesture, and this singer should have a big future on the operatic stage."

Five months later, on 21 April 1941, Johnston returned to Dublin to sing the title role in *Faust,* the opera that he had turned down when it was offered by Colonel O'Kelly. There was one more performance on 25 April, and that ended his association with Dublin Operatic Society because on the formation of Dublin Grand Opera Society, Johnston was offered the role of Alfredo in *La Traviata* on the DGOS opening night on 19 May 1941. The opera was repeated on 23 May, and in the same week he sang the title role in two performances of *Faust*.

Over the next four years until he joined Sadler's Wells, Johnston added to his repertoire the roles of Turiddu (*Cavalleria Rusticana*); Manrico (*Il Trovatore*); Don Ottavio (*Don Giovanni*); and Don José (*Carmen*).

He returned to Dublin many times while he was based in London, and newspaper reports of his four final performance there as Cavaradossi in *Tosca* in November and December 1958, some months after his last appearance at Covent Garden, show that he had lost none of his audience appeal. The title part was sung by Joan Hammond and Otakar Kraus was Scarpia. The critic of the Dublin *Evening Herald* wrote:

> "James Johnston was an heroic Cavaradossi. He sang clearly and forthrightly and cleverly coloured the phrases and acted with vigour. His is the finest Mario we have had in Dublin for a number of years."

The *Evening Mail* said that Johnston's voice had its usual "fine ringing tone."

Johnston chalked up a total of 130 performances in 15 roles in Dublin, Limerick, Cork and Belfast and at Butlin's holiday camp in Mosney, where he sang *Faust* on 12 July 1948, with Dublin Operatic Society and Dublin Grand Opera Society. By the end of 1944 with more than 60 successful operatic performances behind him, he was to be sounded out for a move to the mainland. □

A WINTER'S TALE

In November 1944, James Johnston was singing Don Ottavio in a production of Mozart's *Don Giovanni* with Dublin Grand Opera Society in the Gaiety Theatre, Dublin. It was his last performance of the year and when he returned to Belfast he must have been expecting a recall to Dublin for productions that were scheduled to start in the spring of the following year. But events were to take an unexpected turn which meant that when he next appeared in Dublin more than a year later in December 1945, it would be as a guest, because by then he was a member of the Sadler's Wells Opera Company.

In the winter of 1944-45, Johnston was working in his Belfast shop as usual when he was paid an unexpected visit by Tyrone Guthrie, then the artistic director at Sadler's Wells. During the lean war years, there was a great shortage of tenors and Guthrie was endeavouring to assemble a company to revive opera at the Wells. He had read the Dublin press reports of Johnston's prowess with DGOS and had also had reports from Joan Cross, another director at the Wells, who had appeared with Johnston in Dublin and held him in high esteem. Guthrie decided to travel to Belfast to see whether Johnston would be interested in widening his horizons. He was no stranger to the city, because his first job after leaving Oxford in the early 1920s was with the BBC in Belfast as junior assistant to the director of the new broadcasting station there. His was the first voice on the new 2BE station when it opened on 15 September 1924. Johnston made many broadcasts on local radio, both as a soloist and as a member of the Mayfair Glee Singers quartet, so Guthrie was aware of his singing talent and his popularity.

The scene in the sawdust-strewn shop that winter's day must have been one of great contrasts - the suavely dressed Guthrie, who was over 6ft tall, and the 5ft 7in Johnston, clad in his butcher's apron, working in his shirt sleeves and wielding a meat cleaver. Guthrie walked over to where Johnston was working at his butcher's block.

"Are you James Johnston?"

"Yes, I am", replied the master butcher. "What can I do for you?"

"I'm Tony Guthrie, and I'd like to have a word with you."

Johnston said many years later that his first impression was that Guthrie, the great theatrical producer, must have got the wrong man.

"I can't see why you'd want to see me. Haven't you something to do with the theatre, Shakespeare and that sort of thing?" asked Johnston.

"Yes, but this has nothing to do with Shakespeare. I'm here to talk to you about opera."

"Well, you've got the right man, but I don't think I can help you much. I'm a singer but I'm only an amateur." said Johnston.

"That may be," said Guthrie, "but I've had good reports about you from Dublin, and we'd like you to come and work for us in London, as a professional tenor at Sadler's Wells."

Johnston put down his cleaver, wiped his hands on his apron, and motioned Guthrie to a door that led to a storeroom at the back of the shop. They could continue the discussion there while Johnston's brother Norman, who also worked in the shop, could deal with customers.

"There's no way I could do that," said Johnston, "I'm a great admirer of the people you have over there - Walter Widdop, Heddle Nash - but I don't think I'm in that sort of class. I tell you I'm only an amateur. Anyway, I might not like the life in London."

But Guthrie was not to be put off.

"We could make it a six months trial, for you and for us. If we're unhappy with you or you don't like the life you can come back to Belfast. The pay won't be great to start with, but it's probably more than you earn now."

"Oh no", said Johnston. "I can earn quite a bit on a good Saturday in the shop, but that's not the main consideration. I love to sing and I'll tackle any tenor part, but I don't think I'd fit in with the singers you have there, I'd be out of my class."

"Nonsense", retorted Guthrie. "We have it from Dublin that you're top class, but we need to hear you for ourselves. Let me bring Joan Cross over and you can sing for the two of us and decide after that, but we think you're the man for the job."

Joan Cross arrived with Guthrie a few days later and the trio went to the premises of a local recording company, Hart and Churchill, where Johnston staged an impromptu recital. Guthrie was suitably impressed and Johnston was engaged - but on the strict understanding that there were no ties and that if for any reason he did not like his new surroundings he was free to return to his shop.

When Johnston joined Sadler's Wells towards the end of the war, the company was on tour and performing in Liverpool. In his first professional season Johnston was cast in the role of Jenik in Smetana's opera *The Bartered Bride* in which he made an early impression. The company went to Germany in October 1945 and Johnston appeared in the production in Dusseldorf and at the Berlin Opera House. He also sang Jenik on tour just after the war at the Grand Opera House in Belfast, and the opera was staged again on 20 December 1948 at Sadler's Wells. In that 1945-46 season with the company he also sang Rodolfo, Duke of Mantua, Pinkerton and Turiddu.

Those early performances came to the attention of the Columbia recording company which was inspired to engage him to record Jenik's aria. That was Johnston's first recording, and it was made in 1946 together with his interpretation of *Woman is fickle* from *Rigoletto,* the opera in which he made his debut in Dublin.

In 1946 Sir Malcolm Sargent was in search of a tenor for his forthcoming recording of Handel's *Messiah* with the Liverpool Philharmonic and Huddersfield Choral Society. The oratorio had had its first performance on 13 April 1742 at Neal's Musick Hall, Fishamble Street, Dublin, and it was fitting that Johnston, the man who sang it all over Ireland, should have had the tenor role in the bi-centennial production of the work on 13 April 1942 at Dublin's Gaiety Theatre. The conductor on that occasion was James M. Doyle, the musical director of Dublin Grand Opera Society.

Sargent was aware of the success of that production and knew that, because of his many performances, the oratorio was second nature to Johnston. For his recording, Sargent had engaged the great Lancashire soprano Isobel Baillie, the contralto Gladys Ripley and the bass Norman Walker, who had studied under the Ulster musician Sir Hamilton Harty.

When Johnston was approached to take part in the recording he readily accepted, although he knew that the session in Huddersfield town hall would take several weeks and that he would have to fit in other operatic and concert performances. However, his early experience of the session was not comforting.

The night before he was due to record the recitative *Comfort ye* which precedes *Ev'ry valley,* Johnston was appearing in *Carmen* at Sadler's Wells. After the performance he was collected by Alan Smith, a director of Columbia, and the two left the theatre to catch the late night train to Huddersfield. The travel arrangements had been undertaken by Columbia, so Johnston just boarded the train to which he was directed. Unfortunately it was the wrong one, and it halted for the night at a junction some miles from Huddersfield at about 2 am. There was no transport to Huddersfield at that time of the morning, so Johnston and Smith were forced to await the arrival of the first train later that day. They spent the night on seats on the station platform, in Johnston's words, "shivering and freezing."

They arrived in Huddersfield at about 10 am and before they left the train, Smith told Johnston to head for the hotel and try to get two or three hours sleep and a shower and a shave. He said that he would speak to Sir Malcolm and ask him to go on to some other part of the oratorio. But to their dismay, Sargent was waiting for them on the platform with the news that Isobel Baillie was abroad and that Gladys Ripley and Norman Walker had not turned up.

"Where have you been?" he said to the gaunt Johnston and his companion. "We've been waiting for you; the chorus and orchestra are ready to start."

Smith related the story of the unscheduled stop and remonstrated with Sargent, asking him to allow Johnston to at least have a shower.

"There's no time for that," said Sargent. I can't even allow you time to wash your face. Come on, Comfort ye."

Johnston said many years later that he was "dead beat" when he recorded *Comfort ye*.

"It could have been 100 per cent. better, but Malcolm wouldn't allow any rest. I had to go straight through the piece and that was it. Nowadays singers get several attempts or part of a recording can be re-done and then inserted. But in those days if you made a mistake, even in the last note, the whole thing had to be done again."

In *The Gramophone* of November 1946, the reviewer of the recording wrote of *Comfort ye: Ev'ry valley:*

> "Soloist good, as the day goes. The minutely listening ear can always wish some things better. Tone rather stolid, but the robust tenor is traditional in this part.

"The old hand in the singing world likes to hear the tenor holding his own and being so clear; and I for one can enjoy the Northern pronunciations."

Of the recording as a whole he concluded:

"A bracing experience this *Messiah. Don't miss it!"*

In early November 1946, Sargent conducted a performance of Mendelssohn's *Elijah* at the Royal Albert Hall with the London Symphony Orchestra, Victoria Sladen, Mary Jarred and Johnston, and he called on Johnston again for his recording of that work in 1947. He had again assembled his *Messiah* cast, but this time the bass was Harold Williams. The recording session lasted a month because the members of Huddersfield Choral Society were available only at weekends and evenings, and 10 full recording sessions had to be fitted into that timetable.

At least two thunderstorms of epic proportions occurred during performances, and it was not discovered until later that the sound of the thunder had crept into the recording waxes. As a result, many of the recordings had to be re-made. Like Sargent's *Messiah, Elijah* was also a best seller not only in Britain but in the United States where it was subsequently transferred from 78s to the new 33 rpm LP process, which was available in America for some years before it was introduced here.

Johnston received a letter from the Eastman School of Music in Rochester, New York, congratulating him on the excellence of his performance of the two oratorios. The writer said that the recordings were played to students to demonstrate how oratorio should be sung. The success of the two oratorio recordings led to many concert performances with Sargent and Huddersfield Choral Society at venues all over the British Isles.

In addition to his early success in *The Bartered Bride,* other operas in which Johnston sang the lead at Sadler's Wells included: *Tosca, Cavalleria Rusticana, Madame Butterfly, Rigoletto* and *I Pagliacci.* He also sang *Faust,* and it was said that a night with James Johnston in the title part would sell out Sadler's Wells fast. In 1947, he recorded the love duet from *Butterfly* with Joyce Gartside; *Your tiny hand is frozen* from *La Boheme* and the *Faust All hail thou dwelling.*

A highlight of Johnston's career and one of the operas for which he is best remembered was the 1948 production of Verdi's *Simone Boccanegra.*

The work had never before been presented in Britain, and the cast for its first British performance on 27 October 1948 included: Arnold Matters, who sang the title role; Johnston (Gabriele Adorno); Joyce Gartside (Amelia); Frederick Sharp (Paolo); Douglas Craig (Pietro) and Howell Glynne (Fiesco). The conductor was Michael Mudie, and the production had been translated and adapted by Norman Tucker, the chairman of Sadler's Wells.

The opera was written in 1857 and extensively revised by Verdi 24 years later. For Sadler's Wells it was what one newspaper critic called "a plunge into the operatic unknown" but it was a great success in London. This medieval tale of treachery and passion set in Genoa never attained the popularity of *Rigoletto* or *Traviata* because of its complicated plot and the fact that the hero is not a clear-cut dramatic figure like Rigoletto or Macbeth, but much of its success in that landmark premiere was due to Norman Tucker's excellent simplification of the plot by means of what the critics called his "admirably direct and forceful translation" and the outstanding cast.

For once, the critics were unanimous and described *Boccanegra* as a dramatic and musical masterpiece. *The Listener* said:

"Mr Johnston's ringing tone and urgent delivery came nearest to the true Italianate excitement..."

and *The Scotsman* said that he had, "further enhanced his reputation" and wondered why

"a work of such power and magnificence should have waited 67 years before its revelation to the British public."

Such was the success of the 12 performances of the opera in the 1948-49 season that it opened the 1949-50 season for a further nine performances. It was revived in the 1955-56 season, although by that time Johnston was well established at Covent Garden. But he was invited back to the Wells for the production, which was received just as warmly as the one of some seven years before. Two other members of the cast from the 1948 premiere were in the revived performances, and one critic wrote:

"I thought that in a cast of surpassing excellence James Johnston - borrowed for the occasion from Covent Garden - was outstanding...Here was no lovesick tenor. Mr Johnston's singing and indeed his acting were charged with virility and edged occasionally with vehemence."

For his portrayal of the fiery aristocrat Gabriele Adorno Johnston received consistently good reviews - even for his acting. As we have seen, some 46 years after that British premiere in October 1948, Sir Charles Mackerras still recalls Johnston's

> "marvellous performance...and his noble bearing and heroic voice in the great Aria in Act 111 and in the ensemble in the Council Chamber scene..."

The vital clue to Johnston's acting prowess in that opera is that in a work of "power and magnificence" in which he portrayed a "fiery" character, he had plenty of scope to rise to the occasion. The work has powerfully dramatic music and an outstanding tenor aria, and all those features allowed him to employ the full emotional gamut of his voice. That was where the drama was contained, and stage movements must have been secondary.

Johnston recorded the *Boccanegra* aria in 1948 and it was his favourite recording. It was the one that impressed the Italian experts in Chicago, and Johnston's pleasure at having his recording of the *Song of the Road* from *Hugh the Drover* reissued in the 1970s on the EMI *Record of Singing* collection was tinged with some regret that his great Verdi aria had not been reissued instead. James Shaw recalls that Johnston mentioned that to him some years after the collection had been issued.

> "I told him that the *Song of the Road* was a great recording of an aria that was originally written in English by an English composer, and was therefore eminently suitable for a collection of works in the original language. But he still couldn't quite accept that. I have no doubt that if his *Boccanegra* recording had been in Italian it would have been included. But he never felt comfortable singing in another language, although he frequently did so."

James Johnston made a recording in Italian of *Celeste Aida,* but it was never issued. Those who have heard it will confirm that if he had any worries about singing in Italian they certainly did not show.

On 22 February 1949, close on the heels of his portrayal of Gabriele Adorno, Johnston sang the role of Don José in a new and striking production of Bizet's *Carmen* by the visitor to his Belfast butcher's shop, Tyrone Guthrie. For the production, Guthrie had returned to the novel of Prosper Mérimée whose *Carmen,* in the words of the critic of *Punch,* "is a creature of the gutter, full of the fierce recklessness of the outlaw gipsy folk and of sudden flaming passions that burn out as suddenly as they flare up. She is a being whose very vileness is magnificent."

The reviewer of the production said that its keynote was

"its reeking vitality...paradoxically conveyed by the utmost restraint by producer and designer, and by intense dramatic concentration."

He went on:

"The result is a *Carmen* which few who see will soon forget, and it is achieved without elaborate scenery or costumes, with no ballet and only a small chorus. Mr Guthrie has realised that the music itself is so full of colour that to make colour play an effective part on the stage it must be used as sparingly as possible. The setting of the first act, accordingly, depicting a mean quarter of Seville, is all in black, white and shades of grey, the only touch of colour being provided by the red roses worn by Carmen in her hair and at her waist. In this act the handling of the chorus of cigarette girls is masterly, and succeeds perfectly in suggesting the ugliness of low life and its underlying passion and violence. This comes to the surface in the riot that breaks out when Carmen stabs another girl in a quarrel and again when the girls, hating both Carmen and the men who crowd round her, scream out the words of her song 'If I love you - then take care!' jeering and laughing at Don José as he lies prostrate at the foot of the steps where Carmen in escaping has pushed him.

Acts 2 and 3 are performed in near darkness, the scenery being barely suggested. The dark garden, encircled by a wall, of the tavern of Lillas Pastia is like the evil conspiracy that takes place within it, and like the conflict in the soul of Don José. It throws into relief the braggadocio entry of Escamillo, the toreador song and the truly brilliantly sung quintet by smugglers and their accomplices. The smugglers' den of Act 3 consists merely of an ingenious arrangement of curtains and netting, but in the brooding darkness the card-reading scene becomes a vivid vignette.

If the producer and designer had any doubts about the wisdom of their dark palette for the first three acts, they must have been dispelled by the long-drawn 'Ah!' that the sight of the brilliant colours of the last act drew from the audience as the curtain went up. Here, where the passions of the drama find their climax, is where colour is needed - violent pink, yellow, orange, blue, white, blood-red, gold - and where it tells most. Don José is drunk when he appears, but this, though one dislikes it at first, is in keeping with the general conception, and underlines the degradation into which Carmen's love has dragged him.

The cast suffered badly from first-night nerves, and their intonation suffered accordingly; but Anna Pollak is a very good Carmen and will be better still. James Johnston is a splendid Don José; his voice has developed greatly during the past few seasons...The whole performance is a wonderful display of teamwork..."

That review has been quoted almost in its entirety because not only must it have made pleasant reading for Guthrie and the cast, but it evokes with striking realism the first performance of that acclaimed production of some 45 years ago. *The Times* said:

"Mr James Johnston who is inclined to phlegm, was certainly inspired by Mr Guthrie' dramatic emphasis to convey Don José's distracted passions - he was lyrical in his love song in the second act and powerfully tense in the finale."

Sir Charles Mackerras recently wrote that in many ways, Don José was the greatest of Johnston's roles and recalled that production with "the incomparable Anna Pollak." Johnston was indeed in good company at Sadler's Wells. The roll included such singers as Minna Bower, Marion Studholme, Arnold Matters, the young American soprano Amy Shuard with whom Johnston recorded the Santuzza and Turiddu duet from *Cavalleria Rusticana,* and Olwen Price with whom he recorded Turiddu's farewell from the same opera.

Many of Johnston's colleagues at Sadler's Wells came with him on his frequent visits to Northern Ireland, and were invariably accompanied on concert platforms all over the Province by local singers and musicians, thereby enhancing Ulster's cultural life and providing opportunities that local artists would not otherwise have had. It is not only postwar British opera that owes Johnston a great debt.

In 1958, just a few months before Johnston retired from Covent Garden, he sang his last Don José in his native city in a production of *Carmen,* and in the title part was Anna Pollak. It was fitting that the mezzo-soprano who sang opposite him in so many Sadler's Wells productions should have accompanied him on that occasion.

Some idea of Johnston's versatility and stamina can be gauged from some of his other appearances during that 1948-49 season in which Guthrie's new production of *Carmen* was presented. In just three weeks from 28 September until 18 October 1948, he sang Pinkerton in two performances of Madam Butterfly; the title part in *Faust*; Rodolfo in *La Boheme*; Cavaradossi in two performances of *Tosca*; and Manrico in *Il Trovatore.* Ten days later he sang in the first British performance of *Boccanegra,* and over the next three weeks he appeared in two more, plus two performances of *Tosca* and one each of *Butterfly, Faust* and *Il Trovatore.*

The small Sadler's Wells company was nothing if not innovative, and on 9 May 1950 in the season following the one which saw the first British *Boccanegra* and Guthrie's *Carmen*, they cast Johnston in the title role for a new production of Vaughan Williams's *Hugh the Drover* which had previously been staged by the company in 1939. In a review of the new production in *Opera* of August 1950, Harold Rosenthal wrote:

> "Some would have us believe the work to be an English *Bartered Bride* but Smetana's work translates with ease from Prague to almost any Opera House in the world, and I doubt that this rather naive and adolescent type of stage work would survive even a channel crossing. Despite all this *Hugh* should have a place in our national repertory and receive regular performances...To the title part James Johnston brought something of both the ballad singer (albeit an Irish one) and the operatic tenor, and he is evidently more at ease in the Cotswolds than in the palaces of Mantua; he offered a performance that was nearly always charming and sometimes quite thrilling."

The cast included Joyce Gartside (Mary); Olwen Price (Aunt Jane); Roderick Jones (John the Butcher); George James (The Constable); and Denis Dowling (The Showman). The conductor was James Robertson and the producer and designer, Powell Lloyd, was the

only link with the 1939 production. One critic wrote of that first
night:

> "It is called a 'romantic ballad opera'. Not everyone in the
> Sadler's Wells company has the knack of making the most
> of the delightful ballads; but all fit well into the picture and
> the team, and the famous fight scene in the fairground is
> carried out with robust spirit and effect by James Johnston
> and Roderick Jones, both hefty combatants."

Another critic observed that the acting was "largely non-existent"
and advised Johnston to adopt a more dulcet tone for "his sudden
plunge into romantic love." That comment is reminiscent of his
Dublin reviews in which one commentator was moved to write of
Johnston's performance in *Rigoletto* - "but his lovemaking...oh
dear!"

Johnston's robust spirit and his propensity for practical
jokes - he once told Veronica Dunne that he had concealed a dead
mackerel in Mimi's muff and she was afraid to use it - got him
into trouble with Sadler's Wells over an incident in the fight scene
in *Hugh the Drover*. Roderick Jones, Johnston's rival for Mary's
hand and his opponent in the fight, said that he used to be black
and blue after the encounter in which he and Johnston were
stripped to the waist, because Johnston could not pull his punches.
Hugh the Drover did not interest the cast as much as operas such
as *La Boheme* or *Madame Butterfly,* and they were constantly
seeking ways to revive flagging interest.

At Johnston's suggestion, he and Jones concocted a scheme
on the last night to enliven proceedings, and it was to give Denis
Dowling, who refereed the fight, a punch in the ribs. Dowling
must have been quite unprepared for what was to come, and when
Johnston's punch landed, he fell to the floor and rolled over on to
his face. It was taken by the audience as a joke, but no one knew
at the time that Denis Dowling had sustained three broken ribs.
He was off for six weeks and the management wanted to fine
Johnston six weeks' wages to pay him. But according to Johnston
there were no hard feelings, and Denis Dowling certainly didn't
harbour any because in 1993 he wrote:

> "He was a delightful fellow artist and a hard worker. After
> Sadler's Wells closed down temporarily because of the
> outbreak of war, I was listening to a wireless programme
> from Northern Ireland when I heard a tenor called James
> Johnston. I remember telling my friends that I had never

heard a voice of such quality in this country. When I returned after the war I found that Jimmy Johnston had been a principal tenor at Sadler's Wells for some years. The only two operas we worked in together before he moved to Covent Garden were Hugh the Drover, in which I was the Showman, and Carmen, in which I sang Escamillo.

James's singing and his performances in those and many other leading roles at Sadler's Wells and Covent Garden were of a standard equal to and better than those of many of the world's leading tenors of the day."

During his years in Sadler's Wells, James Johnston built up a huge following and his fans were sorry to see him leave for the larger house. As Sir Charles Mackerras says,

"Although far older than he admitted to, he was immensely attractive to women who used to flock around him after every performance, and his fan mail from young women must have run into several thousands per year!"

Almost all his recordings were made while he was at the Wells but, as is sometimes the case with many singers, recordings do not always do him full justice. It seems that the presence of an audience was Johnston's catalyst - the vital element that enabled him to give of his best. In addition, recording and playback techniques in those days were not up to present day standards: there is a considerable difference between the quality of sound that can be produced by the vibrations of a stylus and that which emanates via a laser beam. The view of James Shaw, who heard Johnston in performance many times in oratorio, in opera and on the concert platform, and who sang oratorio and operatic excerpts with him is that:

"There was a shine, a bloom on his voice in live performances that is sometimes missing in his recordings. Jimmy had a great affinity with his audience, and a charisma that stayed with him throughout his life. He visited me one cold spring day just months before he died, bringing with him all his musical scores. He felt that I might be able to make use of them, and indeed I still do. When he was leaving, my late wife shook his hand at the door, and he grasped it firmly in both hands, looked closely into her eyes and sang, 'Your tiny hand is frozen, let me warm it into life.' I said, 'My boy, there's still a twinkle in your

Top: *Shortly after his debut in* Rigoletto *in Dublin, Johnston sang the title role in* Faust, *the opera that he had initially turned down for Dublin Operatic Society.*

Lower left: *As Lieutenant Pinkerton in an early production of* Madame Butterfly *and (right) as Radames in* Aida *at Covent Garden.*

Top photograph: *Calaf attempting to keep his head in the 1951* Turandot *with Gertrude Grob-Prandl of the Vienna State Opera in the title role.*

Lower left: *With Mme Grob-Prandl in the same production, and* (right) *with Sylvia Fisher before curtain up on the 1957 revival of* Turandot *at Covent Garden.*

Top left: *Johnston's portrayal of Faust was always a great attraction at Sadler's Wells, as was his singing of Calaf* (top right) *in* Turandot.

Lower photograph: *Johnston as Gabriele Adorno and Joyce Gartside as Amelia in* Simone Boccanegra *at Sadler's Wells. Miss Gartside also appeared with him in the much praised revival of* Hugh the Drover.

Top left: *The Bulgarian soprano Ljuba Welitsch whom Johnston had to restrain with a half-nelson during a lively performance of* Tosca.

Top right: *The fine mezzo-soprano Anna Pollak who sang Carmen to Johnston's Don José in the acclaimed Tyrone Guthrie production at Sadler's Wells.*

Lower left: *A later production of* Carmen *at Covent Garden with the American singer Nell Rankin in the title role.*

Lower right: *Johnston as Gabriele Adorno and Arnold Matters as the Doge in a tense scene from the British premiere of* Simone Boccanegra.

eye,' and he said, 'That twinkle will be there until I'm six feet under'."

There are several reasons for the *impression* that Johnston felt more at home in Rosebery Avenue with Sadler's Wells than at Covent Garden, because according to Mrs Johnston he had no qualms at all about singing in either house. In his early, teenage years, he entered competitions all over Ireland and sang at concerts in a myriad of village halls. Hand in hand with those activities went singing in the church choir and his quartet performances and broadcasts. When he graduated to oratorio the halls in which he appeared were not on a scale comparable to London's Covent Garden Opera House. But the size of Covent Garden certainly presented no technical problems. Johnston had a powerful voice and no critic ever complained that it did not carry to the remoter parts of the auditorium.

Nevertheless, Sadler's Wells was smaller than Covent Garden and at least akin to the sort of place to which he was accustomed and would have suited his bonhomie character. When he described Covent Garden Opera House he used the word "massive" and spoke about it with a sense of awe. It is plain that the sheer size of the platform and the auditorium were far removed from his natural element. In addition, the policy of opera in English at the Wells suited him very well. The same policy obtained at Covent Garden for part of his time there, but it was gradually being eroded and he never felt happy singing in Italian.

At Covent Garden there were frequent productions in which artists from abroad appeared and members of the company also sang in Italian. On one occasion in June 1957, Johnston was called in at the last minute to replace Kurt Baum in *Il Trovatore,* and he sang in English while the rest of the cast sang in Italian. Such experiences must have been disconcerting, to say the least.

Allied to those reasons is the fact that Johnston started his operatic career very late. If his father had allowed him to accept the offer of training abroad when he was 19 or 20, his career could have been very different. From that age until his late 30s when he went to sing opera in Dublin - a period of almost 20 years - he continued to work as a butcher and sing as an amateur when he could have been making a name for himself on the international stage. Such a breadth of experience at an early age would have stood him in good stead when, at the age of 47, he stepped on to the Covent Garden stage for the first time.

Although it has been said that Johnston's best performances were in the smaller house, perhaps it would be more correct to say that his best productions were staged there. Sadler's Wells was in good heart to take full advantage of the revival of interest in opera after the war. Its artistic director was Tyrone Guthrie, whose talents as a theatrical director need no elucidation, and the company had such distinguished musicians as Sir Charles Mackerras, Michael Mudie and James Robertson, and Joan Cross and the redoubtable Norman Tucker were but two of its accomplished administrators.

At the end of the war Johnston appeared as a newcomer to British audiences and made an immediate impact as Jenik. In the short space of four years he appeared in the first British production of *Boccanegra,* in a much heralded revival of *Hugh the Drover* and in Guthrie's new and exciting production of *Carmen*. His singing of *Faust* could fill the auditorium, and his oratorio and operatic recordings were best sellers on both sides of the Atlantic. It is little wonder that he is best remembered for his performances at Sadler's Wells.

Almost immediately after the virtually impromptu last-minute appearance with Schwarzkopf in *La Traviata* in January 1949 at Covent Garden, Johnston was offered a place in that company, and he left Sadler's Wells shortly afterwards. He reappeared there frequently as a guest, most notably in the 1955-56 season when he sang again in a revival of *Simone Boccanegra*. His greatest triumphs were in the smaller house, but fine performances lay ahead - notably in *Turandot, Don Carlos*, the Coronation season *Il Trovatore* and *Aida*. □

CORONATION TANTRUMS

The young soprano, who was carrying a little too much weight, had fallen rather heavily. Rehearsals had not started well, mainly because she and Johnston did not always see eye to eye. They were singing well enough together in preparation for the Coronation season production of *Il Trovatore* at Covent Garden, but their personalities could not have been more different. Johnston was inclined to give short shrift to colleagues who engaged in histrionics or who tended to pay too much attention to glowing press reports. His philosophy was that an artist was as good as his next performance: past records were no guide to the future. Not that this young lady was like that - consistency was her hallmark - but he had found to his cost during rehearsals that she had a short fuse.

Perhaps he should not have been quite so rough with a singer who was already acclaimed as the greatest soprano in the world. But according to press reports she was not entirely happy at appearing with "second-rate English singers." If the reports were true, she shouldn't have spoken of colleagues like that; he was no second-rate tenor. Johnston waited for the storm that he was sure would follow when she had picked herself up from the foot of the prop box where he had thrown her.

In that Coronation year of 1953, Johnston's first appearance was as Rodolfo in *La Boheme* in late January, and in early February he sang Radames in two performances of *Aida* in a cast that included Joan Sutherland, Hilde Zadek, Joan Hammond, Gré Brouwenstijn and Constance Shacklock. In mid February that cast from the Royal Opera Company embarked on a two-month nationwide tour, and Johnston again sang Radames in Cardiff, Edinburgh, Glasgow, Liverpool, Manchester and Birmingham. The conductor for the eight performances in which he appeared was Sir John Barbirolli. He sang Gustavus III in *A Masked Ball* with Joan Sutherland and Edith Coates in seven performances in Cardiff, Glasgow, Manchester and Birmingham for which the conductor was Vilem Tausky. On the tour he also sang Manrico in five performances of *Il Trovatore* with Brouwenstijn.

The reviewer in *The Scotsman* said of the Edinburgh Aida:

"James Johnston was not only singing well and sticking to Verdi's marks of expression, but was even articulating the English language as if it was meant to be heard...though no great actor, he gave a thoroughly impressive performance." Within a few days of his return to Covent Garden, Johnston was back singing Calaf with Gertrude Grob-Prandl as Turandot in the production that had opened in late November 1952. In the month leading up to the Coronation he sang Tenor Singer in *Der Rosenkavalier* with Sylvia Fisher, Constance Shacklock, Howell Glynne, Ronald Lewis and Adele Leigh. Now he was busy in rehearsal for the June production of *Il Trovatore* in which he was to sing, in Italian, Manrico to this young and at the moment rather angry Leonora, a singer who was said to be "thrilling the world" and who had made her Covent Garden debut the year before in the title role in Norma - Maria Meneghini Callas.

The *Il Trovatore* cast included Giulietta Simionato, Michael Langdon, Jess Walters and Leonne Mills, and the conductor was Alberto Erede. The first performance was scheduled for 26 June, but the audience on opening night were not to know that, because of the incident at the final dress rehearsal and an obdurate Ulsterman who refused to back down and alter his opinion, Callas was within an inch of refusing to appear.

Johnston was one of the best tenors that the 20th century has produced, but he was also a down-to-earth butcher of Scots-Ulster stock who did not mince words when it came to describing a spade. Such bluntness was in marked contrast to the deferential tone that most people tended to use when addressing Callas.

The two had various differences during preparations for the opera, and matters came to a head at the dress rehearsal shortly before opening night. During the early part of her career Miss Callas was not as trim as she became in later years, and when Johnston was rebuked by the producer for not making the love scenes romantic enough he used to complain, "It's not my fault. I can't get my arms round the flaming woman." Unfortunately, he voiced the complaint while still attempting to embrace his illustrious and somewhat flabbergasted leading lady.

The dress rehearsal was proceeding smoothly until the scene in act lll in which Manrico repels Leonora, believing that she has betrayed him. The production called for Johnston to take hold of Callas and cast her across the stage. In earlier rehearsals he had done so without much force, but as this was a dress rehearsal and he was on stage with a singer whose acting was said to be "electric", he thought it prudent to put some sparkle into it and do it as he would be expected to do it on opening night.

At the end of the two-bar dash heralding the repulse, the stocky Johnston, who was as virile as an ox from his years of handling carcases in his butcher's shop, grasped the hapless Callas by the shoulders, almost lifting her from the boards, and thrust her mightily across the stage. Johnston watched in astonishment as she rolled "like a ball" as he later described it, across the stage and crashed in a mass of flailing arms and legs into the prop box.

There was a moment's silence and the orchestra faded into a series of discordant notes as its members turned their heads first towards the prostrate Callas and then to Johnston, whose face showed wonder at what he thought was electric acting. But he was soon to receive a severe shock. The gallant action would have been to rush to the unfortunate Leonora, help her to her feet, apologise, and continue with the rehearsal. But at that instant the weeks of awkward rehearsals that had gone before were uppermost in his mind, and he ungallantly stood his ground.

Callas, her face flushed with anger, pulled herself laboriously to her feet and glared across the stage.

"How dare you do that to me," she said. "No one does that to Callas."

"Well", said Johnston, "here's one fellow who will, and I"ll do it again on the night - unless you can persuade somebody to change the production, because I'm doing what the producer told me to do."

He said some years later that he did not know that Miss Callas was unaware of the production detail that required him to execute the repulse with such vehemence.

"If you do it again I will leave," said Callas.

"Go ahead, leave if you want to leave. I'd rather sing it with Joan Sutherland, and she can sing it better than you anyway."

When taxed with that comment many years later in a radio interview, Johnston's response was, "Joan Sutherland could sing it better, but the big shots didn't think so."

With that, the rehearsal came to an abrupt end, because Miss Callas promptly left the stage and the theatre.

When Johnston arrived at Covent Garden the next day he was immediately summoned by David Webster, the general administrator, and it was obvious to Johnston that he had had a full report of the incident. In Webster's office, Johnston was asked to relate his side of the story and his defence was that somebody should have told Callas the full details of the production.

"Look, Jimmy," said Webster, deploying his considerable diplomatic skills, "go and see her and apologise. Say you didn't mean to be so rough and it won't happen again. We're only a few days from opening and we have to sort this out."

But Johnston was adamant. If Miss Callas had said, "That was a bit rough," or even "Less of the heavy hand," Johnston's reaction might have been different. But the, "No one does that to Callas" to a man who always spurned airs and graces seemed to rub him up the wrong way.

"I'm not apologising to her. It's not my fault that she wasn't told about the details," Johnston retorted."You can do what you like, David, but as far as I'm concerned I'm ready to go ahead with the first night - with her or without her."

Over the next few days David Webster used all his powers of persuasion on Callas in an attempt to reconcile her to Johnston, but to no avail. Not even dinner at the Savoy had the desired effect. In a desperate last ditch effort he decided to employ a make or break strategem, a move that would completely reconcile the two or drive them irrevocably apart.

On 26 June 1953, just three weeks after the Coronation, Johnston was in his dressing room in Covent Garden putting the finishing touches to his make-up. The auditorium was full and with just a few minutes to go until curtain up, he did not know whether Leonora would be sung by Callas or by an understudy. The door of his room was open and in the mirror of his dressing table he saw the unmistakable reflection of Callas in the open doorway. Without a word she rushed in, threw her arms around him, and planted a kiss on his cheek.

"Thank you, oh thank you, Jimmy," she enthused to a totally bemused Manrico, "I knew I could rely on you."

Before Johnston could collect his thoughts to ask her what she was talking about, she was gone. As Leonora's dressing room was just a few doors along the corridor, he decided to go there for an explanation. Callas was absent, but in the corner of the room there was a huge bouquet with a card attached. Johnston pushed aside some of the blooms and read the inscription.

"To a great artist. I know you will give a wonderful performance. Jimmy Johnston."

On his way back to his dressing room, Johnston met Webster in the corridor.

"Have you spoken to Maria?" asked Webster.

"She's just been to see me and she was all over me. Did you see the flowers in her dressing room, David?"

"Yes. Nice, aren't they?"

"They're lovely, but I didn't send them, although the card on them says I did. Who did send them?"

"I sent them," said Webster. "And I put your name on them." Then coming closer to Johnston he said quietly, "That's what's called diplomacy, Jimmy."

It is not known whether Callas ever discovered the ruse, but it undoubtedly worked because she and Johnston appeared in that *Trovatore* and in two further performances on 29 June and 1 July. The critics described all three as memorable.

As so often happened, some years later, on 13 June 1957, Johnston was called in to sing at short notice - in this case with just three hours to prepare - when Kurt Baum, who had been engaged to sing Manrico to the Leonora of Milanov, came down with a throat infection. Although he had sung the part in Italian in the three performances with Maria Callas in 1953 and again in 1954 with Brouwenstijn, Johnston had no time to revise and sang Baum's part in English while the other members of the cast sang in Italian.

The substitution gave rise to some press controversy as seat prices had been increased to cover the extra cost of the guest singers in the production. The critics observed that it was somewhat lax of the Covent Garden management not to have an understudy for Baum, and the Covent Garden general administrator, David Webster, was drawn into much public correspondence on the issue.

Alongside the brilliance of Callas, Johnston, and indeed the other participants in the 1953 *Il Trovatore* barely rated a mention by the critics, although the correspondent of the *Daily Herald* commented that the performance,

> "was worthy of the best among its predecessors and was marked by some fine singing, in particular by Maria Callas as Leonora and James Johnston as Manrico."

James Johnston's terms of engagement as a permanent member of the Sadler's Wells Opera Company ended in the summer of 1949, although in the absence of a written contract he could have gone immediately on receipt of the offer to join the Royal Opera Company in January of that year, following his unscheduled appearance with Schwarzkopf in *La Traviata*. But he was billed to appear until the end of the 1948-49 season, and from January 1949 until his departure for the larger house, he sang in some 30 performances of *Faust, Butterfly, Tosca, I Pagliacci, Il Trovatore, La Boheme, Carmen,* and of course in the British premiere of *Simone Boccanegra.* Just before his departure he was rehearsing with Sir Charles Mackerras for the part of Babinski in *Schwanda the Bagpipe Player,* a role that he was never to perform.

His first appearance as a member of the Covent Garden company was on 29 September 1949 as Hector de Florac in the first performance of *The Olympians* by J. B. Priestley and Arthur Bliss. The Royal Opera Company had spent £10,000 on the production, a considerable sum at that time, and the cast included Margherita Grandi, Edith Coates, Howell Glynne - who had left Sadler's Wells at the same time as Johnston - Ronald Lewis, Rhydderch Davies, Thorsteinn Hannesson, Shirley Russell and David Franklin. The producer was Peter Brook and the conductor Karl Rankl.

It was the first time for 26 years that a Covent Garden season had opened with a new work by a British composer, and with such talented authors, who were in the audience on the first night, the opera attracted world-wide attention. The full house included executives from La Scala, Milan; the Theatre de la Monnaie, Brussels; the Berlin State Opera and the Paris Opera, and the entire opera was broadcast by the BBC in the Third programme.

But the work received mixed reviews, and while most critics praised its lavishness they had much to say about its many weaknesses, chief of which was the obvious difficulty of fitting the libretto to the music. It was something of a baptism of fire for Johnston, for he disliked it intensely because of the difficulty in keeping the words from breaking the rhythm and flow of the music. The critic of the *Evening News* was in tune with most other commentators when he wrote:

> "It is indeed a mighty theme. Priestley's book, written in a language that makes the average libretto read like a seedsman's catalogue, tells how the pagan gods and godesses, dwindled into a troupe of strolling players,

recover their godhood on midsummer night in 1836 in a French village...The one weakness of the opera is that while it moves with an Olympian majesty, it also moves with an Olympian slowness. One feels that Priestley does not sufficiently realise that words take longer to sing than to speak; and when Priestley gives his characters too many words, Bliss apparently finds difficulty in setting them all to music of equal distinction."

The correspondent of *The Times* praised the opera's "wealth of fine music" and said that it was "a composite work of art in the grand manner." But he continued:

"Too often the actual diction kills not only the poetry but the vocal line...the Olympians should provide a happy hunting ground for debate of the eternal question of words for music. Miss Shirley Russell and Mr James Johnston as the two lovers rightly won chief honours for sheer singing."

Despite that accolade, Johnston was not able to do for *The Olympians* what he had done for *Simone Boccanegra,* because there is no doubt that Johnston's stirring performances in Verdi's opera played a large part in its success at Sadler's Wells. It was fitting that his last appearance at the Wells was in that opera on 11 February 1956 because it was probably one of the works that Lord Harewood had in mind when he said that postwar British opera owed Johnston a great deal. Six years after his appearance in the British premiere it was plain that Johnston had lost none of his flair in the role of Gabriele Adorno. He sang many times as a guest at Sadler's Wells, notably in 1951 and 1953 in new productions of *Hugh the Drover,* another opera for which he was well known.

Reviewers of later productions of that opera by Vaughan Williams still use Johnston's interpretation of Hugh as a benchmark. *The Olympians* had seven performances at Covent Garden in 1949 and was performed three times on tour in the spring of 1950. Thereafter the gods of the work were not seen on earth again.

The late Joan Hammond first sang with Johnston in November 1943 in *Il Trovatore* in Dublin's Gaiety Theatre, and their next appearance together was in the 1950 Henry Wood season. In September, they sang in a radio broadcast of *Der Freischutz,* and were cast together again in 1951 for a new production of *Don Carlos* that opened at Sadler's Wells on 16

January and continued for nine performances. The production had been revived to mark the 50th anniversary of Verdi's death, and the cast included Amy Shuard, Stanley Clarkson and Frederick Sharp. The opera was broadcast on radio, as were many others in which Johnston sang opposite singers such as Brouwenstijn, Anna Pollak and Sylvia Fisher. Sadly, not one recording of those many broadcasts has been preserved. Nothing was ever commercially recorded and nothing exists of Johnston's singing in, for example, *Turandot*, his favourite opera.

In 1951 he appeared with Hammond in *Madame Butterfly* and *Il Trovatore,* and on 19 June of that year Victoria de los Angeles made her British *Butterfly* debut with him, a role that she had sung for the first time in her career just a few weeks earlier in New York. Harold Rosenthal wrote in *Opera* that her performance was "setting a standard" and he went on:

> "The role was sung with consummate taste, the phrasing was impeccable, every nuance being in place...the rest of the cast gave of their very best, and Johnston, Sinclair and Walters were all worthy participants in this memorable evening."

Johnston seems to have had trouble in remembering names, especially if they were foreign - he usually referred to Elisabeth Schwarzkopf, who was married to Walter Legge, as Mrs Legge. Similarly, Mme. de los Angeles was "that nice wee Spanish singer." He was visited in his dressing before curtain up on *Butterfly* by James Shaw, and introduced de los Angeles as, "the wee girl who's singing the title role," and asked her, "What's your name, dear?" He appeared in only a few performances with her, but he followed her career throughout his life and met her when she visited Northern Ireland many years later. As will be obvious from the *Il Trovatore* anecdote, he had a similar affection for Joan Sutherland with whom he appeared many times in *Carmen* and *Aida* at Covent Garden and on a postwar tour of Rhodesia.

What commentators called the "lavishness" of *The Olympians* proved a good introduction to Johnston for his next major role at Covent Garden, that of Calaf in the revival on 22 October 1951 of *Turandot* in which the Austrian soprano Gertrude Grob-Prandl was cast in the title part. Also in the cast were Blanche Turner, Dalberg, Kraus, Rhydderch Davies and Hannesson. The conductor was Sir John Barbirolli, who conducted the first English performance of the opera in 1929 and who was returning to the Royal Opera House for the first time in 14 years. It was a severe test for both principal singers because Johnston had not sung the role before; Mme. Grob-Prandl had just started her professional career; was following in the footsteps of the great English Turandot, Eva Turner, and was singing in English for the first time. Johnston had auditioned for Barbirolli at 24 hours notice before being given the part. Of that first night the critic of *The Times* wrote:

> "Mme Grob-Prandl...has a voice which soars above the leger lines with ease, is true in intonation, and gets richer as it gets higher. Her Princess was an almost credible character because it realised the composer's intentions so truthfully and had the dramatic force of intelligence behind it. Mr James Johnston has the right sort of voice for Calaf, and though the part offers temptations to force the tone, he sang it within his capacity and conveyed the warmth which the Prince must have to thaw the ice of the Princess."

Writing in *Opera,* Harold Rosenthal said:

> "Calaf requires a heroic voice...and also a tenor who can sing the flowing cantilena of the part. James Johnston made a good attempt at the heroics, and for the rest, offered an invigorating and at times exciting performance, which just lacked the requisite power at the climaxes - after all he is no budding Othello; but it was a fine achievement and one of which he may well be proud."

In the summer of that year Johnston sang what was perhaps the most difficult Cavaradossi of his career. Paradoxically, it was the one for which he received the greatest praise. The guest singer for the title role in the June production at Covent Garden was Ljuba Welitsch, a renowned Bulgarian soprano whose promising career was blighted by polyps on the vocal cords. When she appeared with Johnston the condition was already beginning to affect her voice and she adopted various tactics in an attempt to divert attention from her failing powers. In that otherwise all-English performance, Miss Welitsch, who was appearing in the title role for the first time in England, chose to sing not in English or even Italian, which she had done a short time before in New York, but in German.

Throughout the performance she tried to knock Johnston out of his stride by elbowing him in the ribs and stepping on his toes, and when he was lying on the stage she covered his face with her shawl so that he could not see the conductor. Johnston said afterwards: "I wasn't sure what she was up to, but my ribs and feet were painful. Covering my face with her shawl when I was lying on the boards was the last straw. I couldn't see Peter Gellhorn in the orchestra pit, and that made it difficult to follow what was happening.

"I felt I had to take drastic action to stop the performance turning into a shambles, so the next time she approached with her feet and elbows at the ready, I got hold of her by the arm and put her in a half nelson, and that was how we sang the duet.

"After the performance I mentioned her shenanigans to Peter Gellhorn and he said, 'I forgot to tell you about her, she's inclined to do that sort of thing.' I said, 'If I could just have another performance, I would be ready for her.'

"My wife was in the audience and after the performance she said, 'Jim, I have never seen you acting better. You were marvellous.' I said, 'I wasn't acting; I was fighting for my life'."
The Times correspondent wrote:

> "Of Miss Welitsch's supporters, only Mr Johnston as Cavaradossi derived stimulation from the vivid, all too human, portrayal; he sang with greatly enhanced power and musicality, and acted with remarkable fervour."

In November 1951 at the age of 48, Johnston sang Radames for the first time in his career in a concert version of *Aida* at Kingston upon Hull with Amy Shuard and Sir Malcolm Sargent. The opera was one of the big productions in which Johnston always excelled, and he appeared in it at Covent Garden on 1 February with Hilde Zadek, Edith Coates, Rosina Raisbeck and Marian Nowakowski. The guest conductor was Sir John Barbirolli who conducted again in a revival on 14 April.

On that occasion the cast included Gré Brouwenstijn, Constance Shacklock and Jess Walters. James Johnston had what Lord Harewood has called "a direct appeal to an audience", and his singing in the Nile scene always caused a great deal of excitement.

On 2 July 1952 Johnston sang Macduff in a Carl Ebert production of *Macbeth* at Glyndebourne. The opera was in Italian and the international cast included Marko Rothmüller in the title role, Frederick Dalberg, Dorothy Dow, and Philip Lewtas. Of Johnston's performance the *Opera* correspondent wrote:

"Johnston, singing a major role in Italian for the first time in my experience, made a credible figure of Macduff, and his virile singing was refreshingly straight-forward and easy, though he might have identified himself rather more closely with the refugees instead of striding through them to sing his aria as if they were the BBC Chorus at the Albert Hall."

On a lighter note, Johnston's obituarist in *The Daily Telegraph* commented that after the Glyndebourne performance,

"members of the cast who hitched a lift were terrified by the speed with which he drove back to London".

Some mystery surrounds a recording of the Glyndebourne *Macbeth*. An American company, Royale, subsequently published an LP of the opera (LP 1409) on which the names of the performers were changed. On the record Johnston was billed as Horst Wilhelm. So far, efforts to trace the LP have failed. Perhaps a follow-up CD of his recordings —— if one is produced —— will contain that aria from *Macbeth*, if it can be found.

In early 1953 Johnston appeared again in *Aida* in casts that included Sutherland, Zadek, Brouwenstijn, Raisbeck, Shacklock and Rothmüller, and he appeared in three more performances of *Turandot* with Mme Grob-Prandl.

After his differences with Callas during rehearsals for the Coronation season *Il Trovatore,* he was in the firing line again during rehearsals for a new Covent Garden production of *Carmen* in which the title role was to be sung by the American mezzo-soprano Nell Rankin. According to Johnston, Miss Rankin was less than enthusiastic during rehearsals.

Speaking about her many years later, he said that she was "a bit scatterbrained." The cast included another American, Frances Yeend, as well as Joan Sutherland, Ronald Lewis, Michael Langdon and Marko Rothmüller. The producer was Anthony Asquith, but with just six weeks to go until opening night, rehearsals had not proceeded beyond act 1.

The problems came to the attention of the Covent Garden general administrator, David Webster, who approached Johnston in an effort to discover the state of play. Webster did not want to be told what people thought he wanted to hear, and he knew whom to approach for a straight appraisal.

"How is the production going, Jimmy?" he asked. "I've heard about difficulties in rehearsal. Are we on schedule for opening night?"

"You'll never make it," said Johnston. "Tony Asquith is too nice to everybody. People need strong directions and he doesn't want to cause offence. Nell Rankin is very good, but she's a bit giddy and unless she's whipped into shape she won't be able to sing Carmen. We're still on act 1."

"Well what can we do?" said Webster. "What sort of help does she need?"

"The only man who can bring her up to standard is Tony Guthrie," said Johnston, "and he's in charge at Sadler's Wells."

The difficulty presented by that awkward fact was obvious to Webster. There was a deal of dispute at that time between the two companies because Covent Garden had wanted to take over Sadler's Wells as a nursery for budding singers, and Guthrie was adamatly opposed to the idea.

"What about Joan Cross?" asked Webster. "Perhaps a couple of weeks with her would help Rankin."

Guthrie is the best person for the job," said Johnston, "but that's worth a try."

For the next two weeks Nell Rankin was pushed along by Joan Cross and although some progress was made, it was clear that with just a month to go the opera would still not be ready. Webster was finally obliged to call on the services of Guthrie, who arrived in the wings one morning in the middle of rehearsal. He watched quietly until halfway through the duet between Johnston and Rankin, and then stopped the orchestra and walked across to the two principals.

"Miss Rankin, I believe," he said quietly to the somewhat surprised mezzo.

"Yes," she replied, "Nell Rankin."

"It's nice to meet you, Nell", said Guthrie. "You're obviously an American. What part of the States do you come from?"

"Alabama," drawled the young mezzo.

"Well, Miss Rankin", said Guthrie, "please stop waltzing about like an Alabama prostitute and get down to some serious business. Jimmy here is trying his best to make love to you and you are showing no more interest that a dog that's not in heat. If you don't get on with it and do what you're being paid to do, I'll throw you out and get somebody else."

Johnston was never one for mincing words, but even he later expressed surprise as the ferocity of Guthrie's admonishment. But Guthrie's threat had the desired effect and after it rehearsals went smoothly and quickly. Philip Hope-Wallace wrote of the production:

> "Dramatically, only James Johnston's Don José was really up to scratch with a good Flower Song and a tense final five minutes. Nell Rankin did her best...But Carmen wants real acting".

Andrew Porter observed that the production was,

> "stunningly mounted, imaginatively produced, and recreated musically with the utmost finesse",

while Stephen Williams said that Johnston ,

> "filled every phrase with a fine emotional fire."

James Johnston ended 1953 in a production of *Aida* for which Nell Rankin received much better reviews for her portrayal of Amneris. In the title role was Gré Brouwenstijn. The critic of *The Times* commented:

> "Back in the part of Radames, Mr James Johnston was in sufficiently good voice - strong and mellow - to make the importation of any further Egyptian captains from abroad a totally unjustifiable luxury."

On 23 April 1954, Covent Garden staged a revival of *Der Freischütz* in which Johnston had the role of Max to the Agathe of Sylvia Fisher. The cast included Kraus, Walters, Langdon, Geraint Evans and Adele Leigh and the conductor was Edward Downes. It was Johnston's first Covent Garden presentation of the opera, although he had been on tour with it in March and sang Max the year before in a radio broadcast of a concert performance with Joan Hammond. Although he was not to leave Covent Garden until four years later, that was to be one of his last two new roles, the other being Macheath in *The Beggar's Opera* which was staged at Sadler's Wells in October that same year.

He appeared again in *Aida, Carmen, Il Trovatore, Tosca* and *Madame Butterfly* with, among other singers, Hammond, Sutherland, Shacklock, Brouwenstijn, Iacopi and with Rina Gigli, daughter of the great Italian tenor in *Butterfly* at the Dublin Gaiety on 4 May 1954. The correspondent of the Dublin *Evening Herald* said of Johnston's performance in that opera:

> "I have caught most if not all of Johnston's Dublin performances since he began singing in opera here 14 and more years ago, and I have never heard him in finer voice than last evening. He was in supreme control of the role. The phrasing and the attack were faultless, and the voice rode triumphantly and memorably over the immense volume of sound generated by the Radio Eireann Symphony Orchestra under Vilem Tausky."

In 1955, Johnston sang in three revivals: *La Boheme* with Elsie Morison, Geraint Evans and Adele Leigh, *Madame Butterfly* with Amy Shuard and Jess Walters. both at Covent Garden, and in *Boccanegra* with Victoria Elliott, Frederick Sharp, John Hargreaves and Howell Glynne at Sadler's Wells. He also sang with Victoria Elliott in what must have been among the last of his performances as Jenik in a Sadler's Wells production of *The Bartered Bride,* the opera in which he first came to prominence at the Wells. Of his performance in *Turandot* that year Andrew Porter wrote:

> "The hero of the evening was James Johnston whose ringing 'Nessun dorma' prompted the audience to cut into the score with hearty and well-deserved applause."

In 1957, the year before he retired, he appeared in just four operas, one of which was a Covent Garden revival of *Turandot* with Sylvia Fisher in the first Italian role that she had undertaken there, and Amy Shuard. Johnston was his usual ebullient self and, like the throw of Miss Callas, the punch that he failed to pull in *Hugh the Drover* and his arm lock on Welitsch, he struck the palace gong with such vigour on opening night that he knocked it from its fastenings. The critic of *The Times* commented that Calaf "is perhaps James Johnston's finest role" while *The Stage* reported the he was "firm, clear and powerful." He would have been in only three operas that year had it not been for his impromptu singing of Manrico in place of Kurt Baum in the 13 June *Il Trovatore.* Johnston was also in a revival of *The Tales of Hoffmann,* and was singing the role for the first time at Covent Garden. The production opened on 9 July with Veronica Dunne, for whom it was also her first appearance in the role, Mimi Coertse, Barbara Howitt and Otakar Kraus.

On 18 July 1958, James Johnston sang at Covent Garden for the last time in a performance of *Carmen* with Regina Resnik, Joan Sutherland, Monica Sinclair and Richard Lewis, but finished his professional operatic career in Dublin, the city where it had started some 18 years before. On 2 December of that year he sang Cavaradossi in the Gaiety Theatre with Joan Hammond and Otakar Kraus.

In August 1958, the month in which Johnston celebrated his 55th birthday, his voice was still in its prime, but it is fairly obvious from the content and tone of an interview he gave to the *Belfast Telegraph* that thoughts of retirement were in his mind. According to the report he was rehearsing for "a December production of *The Mastersingers*", which would have been the first Wagnerian role of his career. But *The Mastersingers* was not staged by the Royal Opera Company that season, and perhaps Johnston's sudden departure from the Garden had something to do with that because the company had recurring trouble over tenors for the role of Walther.

In January 1957 a new production of the opera opened at Covent Garden, and the role had to be sung by the producer, the German tenor Erich Witte, after Richard Lewis found it unsuitable for his voice and withdrew. It is interesting to note that Witte had to learn English specially for the part as none of the resident Covent Garden tenors - Johnston, Vickers and Edgar Evans - knew the role. On 20 August 1958, a week after his birthday, Johnston sang excerpts from *The Mastersingers* at the Royal Albert Hall during the Henry Wood season and had made a recording of the *Prize Song* some 10 years earlier in 1948.

In his Covent Garden interview for the *Belfast Telegraph* Johnston said:

> "Every year since I came here there's been some up and coming singer who's going to take my place. But I'm still here."

Asked about the fate of singers who were on the "downgrade" he said:

> "they either quit or else take secondary roles, but when I'm not at the top I won't be here."

The reporter astutely observed that Johnston "said it a little defiantly". He also noted that the Belfast tenor was "keenly attached to Ulster."

In the 1959-60 season, Covent Garden again presented *The Mastersingers* and there was more tenor trouble. Ronald Dowd and Edgar Evans shared the first performance when Dowd became ill, Evans singing the *Prize Song* - all he knew of the role - and Witte and the American singer Arturo Sergi, who had taken the role of Walther in a revival of the opera in the 1957-58 season, sang two each of the other performances. Had Johnston not left the company, he might have been able to solve the Royal Opera Company's problems in that 1959-60 production.

Two other factors helped to crystallize Johnston's mind on the issue of retirement. In his last few weeks and for the first time at Covent Garden he was in dispute with David Webster over pay, and it must have been a classic confrontation between two immovables. Secondly and paradoxically, because his voice had the drama to make a great success of the production, the last straw was an offer to sing the heavy tenor roles in a proposed production of Wagner's *Ring*. But when Reginald Goodall told him that he would have to sing in German, Johnston's response was, "No way." He was uncomfortable enough singing in Italian and felt that to launch into a new role in another language would have been too much.

Under the headline:

"James Johnston resigns from Royal Opera Company", the *Belfast Telegraph* of 9 December 1958 reported that Johnston, who was interviewed, appropriately enough, after distributing the prizes at a livestock show and sale in Belfast, said:

> "I had a slight difference of opinion over policy. We parted on good terms. I have many engagements on hand. I had always intended to return to Belfast in any case."

Five years after that interview, in June 1963, Johnston was asked what decided him to retire and he said:

> "There comes a time when you know you have to stop. Time marches on: there's nothing you can do about it. I simply decided on the right moment to come home. There's nothing I have to regret."

His intention on returning to his native city was to teach voice production, and within a short time he had 38 prospective pupils. But he decided against going into teaching, and perhaps it was just as well because he may not have had the temperament to teach. He was not the most patient of men and tact was never one of his strong points.

James Johnston finished his working life in his butcher's shop and although he was in great demand for concerts, he made only rare singing appearances, the most notable of which was in *The Seasons,* a work he had not sung before, in a Belfast performance conducted by Havelock Nelson.

It is sad that James Johnston, the man of humble beginnings who became such a renowned tenor, was accorded no official or civic honour in his lifetime. He was a fine ambassador not only for his native Province but for Ireland, and perhaps typified the archetypal Ulsterman. He is remembered with great affection by all who knew or worked with him, and perhaps the greatest tribute that can be paid to him was expressed by Denis Dowling, a colleague from those early days at Sadler's Wells, who said: "Everybody talks about James with a smile. I could not say anything better than that." ☐

Amy Shuard as Eboli and James Johnston in the title role in **Don Carlos** *in the new production that opened at Sadler's Wells in January 1951. The late Joan Hammond was also in the cast, and the opera was broadcast to commemorate the 50th anniversary of Verdi's death. The recording of the broadcast was not preserved. Later that year Johnston recorded with Miss Shuard the Turiddu/ Santuzza duet from* **Cavalleria Rusticana.**

James Johnston as Don José in Carmen, *one of the many operas in which he appeared. The view of Sir Charles Mackerras is that in many ways Don José was the greatest of all Johnston's roles. He was especially popular in the acclaimed Tyrone Guthrie production at Sadler's Wells.*

JAMES JOHNSTON

An appreciation by Dr. Havelock Nelson

In November 1991 I was privileged to be asked to give an address at a memorial service in St Anne's Cathedral, Belfast, honouring James Johnston. As I recalled in my autobiography "A Bank of Violets", my father allowed me to to to opera matinees at the Gaiety Theatre, Dublin from the age of 10. It was at those some years later that I first heard him on a number of occasions in parts as diverse as Don Ottavio in Mozart's *Don Giovanni* and the Duke in Verdi's *Rigoletto*. At that age I could hardly been fully conscious of the greatness of his voice or his natural artistry but as I listened to it in the cathedral on a recording from an aria from Mendelssohn's *Elijah* 60 years later, it captivated me with its beauty and clarity and sent shivers up my spine, a sign of its outstanding quality.

Those early visits to the opera reminded me of my next encounter with Jimmy when I was in my late teens as organist in the Centenary Methodist church in Stephen's Green. The choir mistress was a beautiful and talented woman called Sylvia Fannin and she conducted a performance of the *Messiah* every year at Christmas for which I played the organ. There were only two tenors in her opinion - one was James Johnston and the other was Peter Pears, a very different kind of artist. Both of these I was to meet and work with many times in the future in my musical career.

By the time I came to live in Belfast in 1947 to work in the BBC, Jimmy was well established in London, first at Sadler's Wells and later at Covent Garden. Our first performance together was a concert version of *Hugh the Drover* by Vaughan Williams with which Jimmy had had a personal success in Sadler's Wells when he sang the title role. On this occasion I conducted it in the Assembly Hall with the Ulster Singers which had been formed by Jimmy's singing teacher, John Vine, whom I succeeded on his retirement. The present director of Opera Northern Ireland, Kenneth Montgomery, was present as a schoolboy at the performance and was able to record his enthusiasm.

During the years when James Johnston lived in London, he was a constant guest artist at the various Saturday night choral concerts which were a feature of musical life at that time.

Needless to say, any concert promoter was assured of a full house if he starred.

On one occasion he rang me on the morning of a concert to say that there was a London fog and would I ask a young Cathedral tenor called Joe McCartney, whom he had helped vocally occasionally, to stand by "just in case-". So Joe sang in the first half and when I came back to the Green Room at the interval Jimmy was sitting waiting for me. He *had* arrived on time but stayed hidden so as not to spoil Joe's "hour of glory"! What's more, he insisted on Joe singing in the second half as well as himself! The audience loved every minute of it, even though they didn't get out of the hall till midnight.

At the launching in 1958 of the Grand Opera Society of Northern Ireland, Jimmy sang Don José in *Carmen,* which I conducted. In spite of various teething troubles he remained helpful and co-operative; no temperamental tenor hysterics!

When Jimmy eventually returned to live in Belfast he refused many offers for concerts here. However, because of his past connection with the Ulster Singers, he agreed to take part in Haydn's *The Seasons* which he had never sang before. We worked together for a month and he gave a splendid performance on the night. I still think that he was the best tenor I ever heard in *The Creation.* After that he really *did* retire but our paths crossed periodically on various occasions. I remember a "This is your life" kind of programme broadcast by RTE and featuring Veronica Dunne with whom he had sung many times. Each of them tried to outdo the other with their stories of operatic mishaps.

All of us who worked with Jimmy can never forget the vitality and beauty of his voice, his natural artistry and the incredible clarity of his words. Had he lived in the period of the 1970s or 1980s he would have been snowed under with recording contracts. As it is the few recordings that he made are treasured by his many admirers as mementoes of a truly great voice and musical personality. □

Dr. Havelock Nelson, OBE is one of Ireland's most distinguished musicians. He worked with the BBC Northern Ireland, the Ulster, National Symphony and RTE orchestras. Conducting and adjudicating engagements have taken him to Europe, Canada, the Far East and the West Indies. On piano he has accompanied Peter Pears, Leon Goosens, James Galway and Jack Brymer. He is a Fellow of the Royal Academy of Music.

THE BASS IN SHORTS

by Leslie McCarrison
(Rathcol of the Belfast Telegraph)

Like so many male singers, James Johnston had his first experience of vocal art in a church choir, but not in the traditional role of a choirboy. At the suggestion of a youth leader at the Methodist church he attended, he agreed to join the adult choir in which, as he put it years later, "I was a 15-year-old in shorts singing bass."

At a music festival in Ballymena, County Antrim, James Johnston was advised by the adjudicator in the baritone class to start singing tenor, and although at first he rebelled, he soon found that the suggested change was to have a profound influence on his life.

His next important move was to the choir of St. Anne's Cathedral in Belfast, where he became one of the two paid tenors. His opposite number, Mr. R. M. Kent, a native of Durham, was also a splendid lyric tenor and had several offers, which he turned down, to join the Carl Rosa.

Johnston said that his first solo in the cathedral choir was not good and, as a conscientious young man, he offered his resignation to the director of music, C. J. Brennan. Refusing to accept it, Brennan told him, "Now you know what you are up against."

James never forgot his cathedral training, which was invaluable when he started to sing in operatic ensembles. As he put it, "It wasn't what they paid me, it was what they taught me that counted."

Although the Belfast-born tenor was tremendously popular in Ireland, and an essential ingredient of top performances of oratorios such as the *Messiah* and *Elijah*, he had little difficulty in coming to terms with singing opera, and particularly the great Italian tenor roles, although he never professed to be a great actor. The "Concise Oxford Dictionary of Opera" hit the nail on the head when it stated that "he sang Italian roles with a ringing tone and intensity rare among British singers."

Although Johnston was in the cast of Verdi's *Macbeth* at Glyndebourne, it appears that the conductor Vittoria Gui had originally wanted a foreign artist. But Equity refused to countenance that, insisting on the employment of a British singer. James told me that, at the outset, the conductor was not particularly easy to work with, but that he was advised not to yield an inch, and common sense won the day.

Few people know that James was offered the part of Riccardo in Glyndebourne's Edinburgh production of *Un Ballo in Maschera*. As it was to have 11 performances, it was decided to have alternative casts of the major principals, but Johnston refused to join the second cast because he considered - and rightly, too - that he was a far better tenor than Mirto Picchi in the first cast.

Honesty was always an endearing characteristic of James Johnston, and when he later met the splendid soprano, Margherita Grandi, who was playing second to Ljuba Welitsch in the first cast, he agreed with the Tasmanian artist that he had been "very naughty."

As a teenage organist and a member of St. Anne's Cathedral Youth Group, I got to know James Johnston just prior to his London debut, and throughout his life he never forgot the stage-struck younster, taking me and a friend to Glyndebourne for rehearsals. It was an unforgettable experience.

James's stories about his life abounded, and I particularly relished his description of the *Messiah* which he recorded with Sir Malcolm Sargent. The conductor wanted the tenor to make one or two changes in his approach to *Comfort Ye* and *Ev'ry Valley*, and they took some time to sort out.

In those days, 78 rpm recordings were made directly on to wax formers, and a number of those had to be discarded to allow for "fluffs". At last a recording without a slip was nearing completion when suddenly someone on the roof dropped a hammer.

It was decided to have yet another go and, as James was in top form, he did not put a foot wrong. I asked him how that was achieved and, with a grin, Jimmy confided that just before they commenced he promised that he would buy every member of the orchestra a drink if he made any more mistakes. Said James, "That put the fear of God into me!"

Sir Malcolm Sargent, who had a high regard for Johnston's singing, put the cat among the pigeons when he decided to displace the then reigning British oratorio tenor, the excellent Heddle Nash, for his complete *Messiah* recording, replacing him with the Irish contender for the crown.

James was over the moon at the honour, and I remember his bemused reaction when he was told that, on hearing that he had been dropped, Nash exclaimed: "And me the best bloody Messiah in England." Sargent apparently refused to be drawn into any argument, merely stating that he had opted for a younger singer.

Apart from his appearance in Belfast with the Grand Opera Society of Northern Ireland, James also made a brief appearance in the city with the Dublin Grand Opera Society when he sang Alfredo in a production of *La Traviata*.

The Grand Opera Society of Northern Ireland was founded by local singing teacher John Patterson and John Lewis-Crosby as a means of filling the vacuum left by the loss of the visits by the Carl Rosa Opera, at the time owned by Mrs Philips from Londonderry - who took over the reins of management on the death of her husband Mr. H.B. Philips.

John Patterson, who studied singing in Italy, had been a principal with the Rosa, whose fine chorus consisted mostly of his pupils. John Lewis-Crosby also had a long association with the arts, and had also studied singing on the continent. His partnership with John Patterson proved excellent. It is interesting to note that most of the GOSNI productions were mounted in conjunction with an Italian-based impressario, who offered a package deal of principals, producer and conductor, scenery and costumes for each opera. Anna Moffo sang the society's first Gilda, and in the cast of the first never-to-be-forgotten staging in Belfast of *Madame Butterfly* was an unknown tenor making his first appearance outside Italy, prior to going to Dublin and then Covent Garden. His name was Luciano Pavarotti.

After the war, the first visit of the Sadler's Wells Opera Company to Belfast was greeted with enthusiasm, especially when it was known that their latest recruit, Belfast-born James Johnston, would be among the company.

Our delight knew no bounds when it was known that he would be heard as Jenik in that most delightful of operas, Smetana's *The Bartered Bride*, but there was a snag: the opera company management, presumably Joan Cross, refused to issue cast lists, and there was bitter disappointment when it was discovered that the local lad had been left out of all review performances, but was appearing in the second cast. Local scribes got round the difficulty by bribing members of the ballet to locate "Johnston nights" for us, and we remember the roar of laughter when the Marriage Broker (Owen Brannigan) asked Jenik, "And who might you be?", he was told in an unaltered Belfast accent, "I'm a stranger in these parts."

Early in his operatic career James Johnston vowed, "When I feel that I'm not singing up to the standard I expect, I'll quit. I want people to say, 'Why did Johnston not stay on?' rather than, 'Why did he not go when he was good?'." He kept that promise, returning to the butcher's shop in Sandy Row where he had been discovered, and which he insisted on being kept on against his retirement. He was a gentleman and a real friend to the many young, aspiring singers who crossed his path. □

PERFORMANCE LIST

The dates of Johnston's performances for Dublin Grand Opera Society and the Royal Opera Company are complete. Casts have been compiled from programmes, where these were available, and from lists of forthcoming productions, and in most cases apply only to initial performances.

Performances and cast lists for Sadler's Wells have been compiled almost entirely from lists of forthcoming productions, which for 1944-45 and for 1945-46 are missing. Where available, programmes have been used. Newspaper and magazine reviews have filled some gaps but many remain, especially on his oratorio and concert performances.

The list is the result of many months of work, and time constraints did not allow a more detailed investigation. It is hoped that those who have additional information on James Johnston's performances will be willing to supply it so that the list can be made as complete as possible.

1940
Rigoletto (Duke of Mantua); May Devitt, Geraldine Costigan, John Lynskey, Jack Harte, cond. E. Godfrey Brown; Dublin Gaiety: 25 Nov., (operatic debut) 30 Nov., 5 Dec.

1941
Faust (Faust); Elizabeth Sheridan, Harte, W. Lemass; Dublin Capitol: 21, 25 April. With Helen Paxton, Patricia Black, Lynskey, Irwin; Dublin Gaiety: 22, 25 May; Limerick Savoy: 5 June. With May Devitt, Black, J. C. Browner; Dublin Gaiety: 8, 14 Nov.

La Traviata (Alfredo); Devitt, Robert Irwin; Dublin Gaiety: 19 May (opening night and first performance by the newly-formed Dublin Grand Opera Society); 23 May; Limerick Savoy: 2, 6 June. With Renee Flynn, N. J. Lewis; Dublin Gaiety: 4, 15 Nov.

Cavalleria Rusticana (Turiddu); Black, Sam Mooney; Dublin Gaiety: 6, 10, 13 Nov.

Rigoletto (Duke of Mantua); Moira Griffith, Lynskey; Dublin Gaiety: 11 Nov.

1942

Messiah; Rita Lynch, Black, Hooton Mitchell; Dublin Gaiety: 13, 19 April, and on 20 Dec. with Mabel Thrift, Black, Richard Mason.

Il Trovatore (Manrico); Griffith, Black, Lynskey, Mooney; Dublin Gaiety: 15, 21 April.

Cavalleria Rusticana (Turiddu); Griffith, Mooney; Dublin Gaiety: 18, 23 April; Cork Opera House: 6, 9 May.

La Traviata (Alfredo); Cork Opera House: 4, 9 May; Dublin Gaiety: 2, 12 Dec.

Faust (Faust); Cork Opera House: 7 May.

1943

Faust (Faust); Devitt, Black, Browner, Sean Mooney; Dublin Gaiety: 5, 10 May.

Don Giovanni (Don Ottavio); R. Flynn, R. Lynch, Marie Slowey, Michael O'Higgins, Sam Mooney; Dublin Gaiety: 8. 12, 15, 17 May.

Il Trovatore (Manrico); Joan Hammond, Black, R. Mason, Sam Mooney; Dublin Gaiety: 17, 26 Nov.

The Bohemian Girl; Lynch, Browner, Black, Sam Mooney; Dublin Gaiety: 23, 27 Nov.

1944

La Traviata (Alfredo); Flynn, Lynskey; Dublin Gaiety: 17, 22, 26 April; Cork Opera House: 1, 6 May.

Il Trovatore (Manrico); Griffith, Black, Mason; Dublin Gaiety: 18, 28 April; Cork Opera House: 4 May.

Faust (Faust); Flynn, Black, Browner, Mason; Dublin Gaiety: 20, 24, 29 April. With Devitt, Black, Browner; Cork Opera House: 3, 7 May.

Rigoletto (Duke of Mantua); Marion Davies, Lynskey; Dublin Gaiety: 20, 25, 30 Nov.

Carmen (Don José); Black, Lynskey; Dublin Gaiety: 22, 27 Nov., 2 Dec.

Don Giovanni (Don Ottavio); Flynn, Lynch, Slowey, O'Higgins, Sam Mooney; Dublin Gaiety: 24, 29 Nov.

1945

Madame Butterfly (Pinkerton); cond. Goodall; Grand Opera House, Belfast: 27 July.

Concert; Tonypandy: 18 Oct.

Bartered Bride (Jenik); Minna Bower, Edmund Donlevy, Peter Pears, cond. Goodall; Grand Opera House, Belfast: 30 July. With Gilbert Bailey, Olwen Price, Victoria Sladen, Owen Brannigan, cond. Süsskind; Berlin: 1 Oct., Dusseldorf: cond. Goodall, 26 Oct.

Faust (Faust); Victoria Sladen, Roderick Jones; Dublin Gaiety: 26 Nov., 1, 5 Dec.

Il Trovatore (Manrico); Ruth Packer, P. Black, Lynskey, R. Mason; Dublin Gaiety: 27, 29 Nov., 1 Dec.

Rigoletto (Duke of Mantua); Linda Parker, Kate Jackson, Roderick Jones, Owen Brannigan, Catherine Lawson, Gilbert Bailey, cond. Goodall; Berlin Opera House: 2 Oct. With Gwen Catley, Roderick Jones; Dublin Gaiety: 4, 6, 8 Dec.

1946

La Boheme (Rodolfo); cond. Collingwood; Sadler's Wells: 23 Jan.

Concert, Whitehall Theatre, London: 14 April.

Cavalleria Rusticana (Turiddu); Monica Warner, Ruth Packer, Olwen Price, Ivor Evans, cond. Clayton; Sadler's Wells: 2 May.

Faust (Faust); Belfast Hippodrome: 17, 19, 21 Sept.

Elijah; Victoria Sladen, Mary Jarred, Harold Williams. LSO, cond. Sargent; Royal Albert Hall: 2 Nov.

Tosca (Cavaradossi); Sybil Lloyd, Ivor Evans, Victoria Sladen, Roderick Jones, Olwen Price, cond. Mudie; Sadler's Wells: 18 Dec.

1947

Cavalleria Rusticana (Turiddu); Packer, Shires, Olwen Price, Llewellyn, Pollak, cond. Mudie; Sadler's Wells: 22 Jan., 5 Feb., 16, 19, 21, 24 April, 2, 7, 10 May.

Tosca (Cavaradossi); Jackson, Sladen, R. Jones, D. Jones, Evans, Llewellyn, cond. Mudie; Sadler's Wells: 3, 8, 14, 19, Feb., 17, 26 March., 2, 5, 10 April, 13, 16 Sept., 7, 22 Oct.,13, 22 Nov., 10 Dec. With Sladen, R. Jones; Dublin Gaiety: 8 Dec.

Bartered Bride (Jenik); Bower, M. Jones, Glynne, cond. Mudie; Sadler's Wells: 12, 15, 17, 20, 28 Feb., 5, 8, 10, 13, 20 March, 7 April, 26 Sept., 2, 21, 27 Oct., 26 Dec.

Madame Butterfly (Pinkerton); Sladen, Iacopi, R. Williams, Llewellyn, cond. Mudie; Sadler's Wells: 22, 25 Feb., 20, 24 Sept. With Sladen, Glynne; Belfast Hippodrome: 28, 29 Oct.

Concert; Duet from *Bartered Bride* with Howell Glynne; Quartet from *Rigoletto* with Veronica Sladen, Anna Pollak, Roderick Jones; Duet from *La Boheme* with Sladen; Solo: *All Hail thou dwelling; Faust* trio, with Sladen and Glynne; Royal Albert Hall: 9 March.

Carmen (Don José); P. Black, George Hancock; Dublin Gaiety: 29 April, 3, 6, May.

Rigoletto (Duke of Mantua); Terry, Pollak, Matters, Glynne, cond. Mudie; Sadler's Wells: 3, 9 May, 4, 10 Oct. With Gwen Catley, Leyland White; Dublin Gaiety: 1 May.

La Boheme (Rodolfo); Blanche Turner, Josephine O'Hagan, L. White, Owen Brannigan; Dublin Gaiety: 8, 10 May.

Faust (Faust); Lowe, Pollak, O. Price, Roderick Jones, Glynne, cond. Mudie; Sadler's Wells: 14, 18, 24 Oct., 6, 17, 26, 28 Nov., 1, 3, 9, 23, 31 Dec.

La Traviata (Alfredo); R. Packer, R. Llewellyn; Belfast Hippodrome: 28, 29 Oct.

I Pagliacci (Canio); Bower, Llewellyn, Sharp, cond. Mudie; Sadler's Wells: 14, 20, 29 Nov., 1, 3 Dec.

Messiah; Olive Groves, Nancy Evans, Owen Brannigan, Huddersfield Choral Society, cond. Sargent; BBC broadcast from Huddersfield town hall: 19 Dec.

1948

I Pagliacci (Canio); Bower, Roderick Jones, Sharp, cond. Mudie; Sadler's Wells: 5, 20 Jan., 9, 19 Feb., 6 March, 17 May, 29 Dec.

Madame Butterfly (Pinkerton); Joyce Gartside, Pollak, Roderick Jones, cond. Robertson; Sadler's Wells: 8 Jan., 4, 23 Feb., 19, 23 April, 8 May, 1, 12 Oct., 6 Nov., 2, 14, 30 Dec.

Tosca (Cavaradossi); Jackson, Roderick Jones, D. Jones, cond. Mudie; Sadler's Wells: 12, 29 Jan., 13 Feb., 17, 26 April, 14 May, 8, 18 Oct., 4, 20 Nov., 22 Dec.

Faust (Faust); Lowe, Pollak, O. Price, Sharp, Glynne, cond. Robertson; Sadler's Wells: 15, 24 Jan., 2 Feb., 2 March, 9, 22,

28 April, 6, 10, 22 May, 28 Sept., 8, 30 Nov., 8 Dec. With M. Field, Joyce Nelson, Henry Gill, Bruce Dargavel; Dublin Gaiety: 1, 5 May. With Field, Black, Harvey Allen, Dargavel; Mosney: 12 July.

La Boheme (Rodolfo); Field, Barbara Lane, J. Lynskey, Dermot Browner; Dublin Gaiety; 3 May. With Lowe, Jackson, Roderick Jones, Donlevy, cond. Mudie; Sadler's Wells: 6 Oct., 6 Dec.

Il Trovatore (Manrico); Gartside, Price, Sharp, Clarkson, cond. Mudie; Sadler's Wells: 15 Oct., 17 Nov., 16 Dec.

Simone Boccanegra (British premiere) (Gabriele Adorno); Gartside, Matters, Sharp, Craig, Glynne, cond. Mudie; Sadler's Wells: 27, 30 Oct., 11, 24 Nov., 10 Dec.

Rigoletto (Duke of Mantua); Joan Butler, J. Lynskey; Dublin Gaiety: 29 April. With Shires, Pollak, Roderick Jones, Glynne, Alan, cond. Robertson; Sadler's Wells: 27 Nov.

Bartered Bride (Jenik); Shires, Kentish, Glynne, cond. Quayle; Sadler's Wells: 20 Dec.

1949

Faust (Faust); Gartside, Pollak, Price, Roderick Jones, Glynne, cond. Mudie; Sadler's Wells: 5 Jan., 12 May, 24 Nov. With Gartside, Black, D. Brannigan, R. Jones; Dublin Gaiety: 29 April, 2, 4 May.

Simone Boccanegra (Gabriele Adorno); Gartside, Matters, Sharp, Craig, Glynne, cond. Mudie; Sadler's Wells: 7. 21 Jan., 9 Feb., 4, 19, 29 March, 21 April, 9 May.

La Traviata (Alfredo); Elisabeth Schwarzkopf; Covent Garden: 11 January.

Concert, with Tara Barry, Robert Irwin, Joan and Valerie Trimble, Ronald Settle; Liverpool: 14 March.

Concert, with Gwen Catley, cond. Vic Oliver; Earl's Court: 27 March.

Madame Butterfly (Pinkerton); Gartside, Pollak, Sharp, cond. Mudie; Sadler's Wells: 12, 17 Jan., 12 Feb., 28 March, 26 April. With Korina Hellas, Melvyn Bartell; Dublin Gaiety: 6, 7 May.

Tosca (Cavaradossi); Sladen, Matters, Craig, cond. Mudie; Sadler's Wells: 14 Jan., 2, 28 Feb., 2, 19 April. With Doris Doree, Otakar Kraus; Dublin Gaiety: 9 Dec.

I Pagliacci (Canio); Shires, Roderick Jones, Craig, cond. Mudie; Sadler's Wells: 19 Jan., 5 Feb.

Il Trovatore (Manrico); Gartside, Boardman, Roderick Jones, Clarkson, cond. Mudie; Sadler's Wells: 24 Jan., 11, 23 March, 11 April. With Doree, P. Black, Dargavel, Jack Harte; Dublin Gaiety: 6, 8, 12 Dec.

La Boheme (Rodolfo); Lowe, Bower, Matters, Donlevy, Allen, cond. Robertson; Sadler's Wells: 31 Jan., 15 Feb., 23 April, 5 May.

Carmen (Don José); Bower, Pollak, Roderick Jones, cond. Mudie; Sadler's Wells: 22, 26 Feb., 9, 17, 21 March, 7, 16, 25 April, 14 May, 6 Nov.

Rusalka (Prince); Gré Brouwenstijn, Rosina Raisbeck, Anna Pollak, cond. Stanford Robinson; BBC broadcast (first performance in English): 1 April.

Cavalleria Rusticana (concert performance) (Turiddu); Victoria Sladen, Roderick Jones, Anna Pollak, Olwen Price, cond. Groves; BBC broadcast: 29 July.

Henry Wood concert; excerpts from *The Mastersingers* with Victoria Sladen, Marjorie Thomas, Murray Dickie, Tom Williams, cond. Cameron, LSO: 8 August.

The Olympians (First performance)(Hector de Florac); Murray Dickie, Edith Coates, Ronald Lewis, Howell Glynne, Shirley Russell, Rhydderch Davies, Thorsteinn Hannesson, Margherita Grandi, Kenneth Schon, cond. Karl Rankl; producer, Peter Brook; Covent Garden: 29 Sept., 7, 18, 24, Oct., 1, 29 Nov., 22 Dec.

1950

Carmen (Don José); Lowe, Pollak, Probyn/Roderick Jones, cond. Mudie; Sadler's Wells: 5, 17, 26 Jan., 27 Feb., 8 March, 17, 25 April, 25 Sept., 4, 18, 23 Oct.With Coates, Blanche Turner, Bowman, Raisbeck, Geraint Evans, cond Gellhorn: Covent Garden: 26 May. With Martha Modl, G. Evans, Raisbeck, cond. Rankl; Covent Garden: 2, 30 Nov.

Faust (Faust); Gartside, Proust, Black, Sharp, Glynne, cond. Quayle; Sadler's Wells: 7, 24, 30 Jan., 15 Feb., 10 April.

Il Trovatore (Manrico); Gartside, Black, Sharp, Alan, cond. Robertson; Sadler's Wells: 10, 20 Jan., 10 Feb. With Serafina di Leo, P. Black, B. Dargavel; Dublin Gaiety: 19 Dec.

Simone Boccanegra (Gabriele Adorno); Sladen, Roderick Jones, Probyn, Clarkson, cond. Mudie; Sadler's Wells: 7, 23 Feb.

Madame Butterfly (Pinkerton); Sladen, Black, Roderick Jones, cond. Robertson; Sadler's Wells: 13 Feb. Royal Opera House tour: 11, 18 March, 1, 22, 29 April. With Hammond, Sinclair, Williams, cond. Braithwaite; Covent Garden: 17 Nov., 12, 27 Dec.

Verdi's Requiem; Sylvia Fisher, Rosina Raisbeck, Trevor Anthony, cond. Sargent; Liverpool Philharmonic Hall: 25 Feb.

The Olympians (Hector de Florac); Royal Opera House tour: 10, 24 March, 21 April.

Hugh the Drover (Hugh) (new production); Gartside, Price, Roderick Jones, James, cond. Robertson; Sadler's Wells: 9, 12, 17, 20 May, 21, 29 Sept., 21, 25 Oct.

Concert, with Bruce Dargavel, Lorely Dyer, cond. Stanford Robinson; Bournemouth: 18 June.

Henry Wood prom., operatic excerpts; Hammond, cond. Stanford Robinson; Royal Albert Hall: 5 Aug. Wagner concert, cond. Sargent, 6 Sept.

Der Freischutz (Max); Hammond, Ian Wallace, Adele Leigh, cond. Stanford Robinson; BBC broadcast: 22 Sept.

La Traviata (Alfredo); Schwarzkopf, Walters, cond. Gellhorn; Covent Garden: 20 Oct. With Schymberg, 2 Dec.

Der Rosenkavalier (Tenor Singer); Clifford, Fisher, Glynne, Jones, Graf, Shacklock, Schwarzkopf, cond. Rankl/Kleiber; Covent Garden: 23 Nov., 6 Dec.

Rigoletto (Duke of Mantua); Coates, Nowakowski, Williams, cond. Gellhorn; Covent Garden: 28 Nov.

Tosca (Cavaradossi); Covent Garden: 4 Dec.

I Pagliacci (Canio); Bower, R. Jones, Arthur Copley; Dublin Gaiety: 5, 14, 16, 17 Dec.

1951
Der Rosenkavalier (Tenor Singer); Clifford, Fisher, Glynne, Graf, Jones, Shacklock, Watson, cond. Kleiber; Covent Garden: 4, 20 Jan.

Messiah; Ada Alsop, Margaret McArthur, Harold Williams, cond. Sargent; Royal Albert Hall: 6 Jan.

Don Carlos (new production) (Don Carlos); Hammond, Shuard, Sharp, Clarkson, Alan, cond. Mudie; Sadler's Wells: 16, 19, 24, 27, 29, 31 Jan., 5, 14, 30 May.

Madame Butterfly (Pinkerton); Hammond/Turner, Sinclair, Williams, cond. Braithwaite; Covent Garden: 22 Jan., 5, 14 Feb., 12, 20 April. With de los Angeles, Sinclair, Walters, cond. Braithwaite; Covent Garden: 19, 27 June. Royal Opera House tour: 20 March.

Il Trovatore (revival) (Manrico); Dora Drake, Clarkson, Price, Sharp, cond. Mudie; Sadler's Wells: 8, 12, 17, 23 Jan., 11, 23 Feb., 3, 13 March. With Coates, Hammond, Nowakowski, Walters, cond. Gellhorn; Covent Garden: 3 Feb., 2, 17 April. With Brouwenstijn, Coates, Langdon, Walters, cond. Capuana; Covent Garden: 18, 22 Dec. With Franziska Petrie, P. Black, Dargavel; Dublin Gaiety: 13 Dec.

Hugh the Drover (Hugh); Gartside, Price, Probyn, James, cond. Robertson; Sadler's Wells: 10, 23 Feb., 12, 23 May.

Carmen (Don José); Graf, Raisbeck, G. Evans, Shacklock, cond. Kleiber; Covent Garden: 15 Feb. With Gartside, Pollak, Probyn, cond. Mudie; Sadler's Wells: 25 Nov. With Black, Dunne, R. Jones; Dublin Gaiety: 19 Dec.

Simone Boccanegra (Gabriele Adorno); Houston, Matters, Probyn, Glynne, cond. Robertson; Sadler's Wells: 28 Feb., 10, 22 March, 9, 28 May, 9 June, 11 Oct., 3 Nov.

La Traviata (Alfredo); Royal Opera House tour: 9, 30 March. With Schymberg, Walters, cond. Gellhorn; Covent Garden: 4, 19 April.

Faust (Faust); Lowe, Pollak, Price, Sharp, Alan, cond. Quayle; Sadler's Wells: 28 March. With Veronica Dunne, Patrick Lawlor, Glynne, Dargavel; Dublin Gaiety: 4, 6 Dec.

Tosca (Cavaradossi); Kraus, Zadek, cond. Gellhorn; Covent Garden: 3 April, 1 May. With Ljuba Welitsch, Rothmüller, cond. Gellhorn; Covent Garden: 23, 28 June. With Grandi, Kraus, cond. Capuana; Covent Garden: 19, 27 Nov., 10 Dec. Royal Opera House tour: 17, 21, 24 July.

La Boheme (Rodolfo); Victoria Elliott, Jess Walters; Dublin Gaiety: 24, 26 May.

Rigoletto (Duke of Mantua); Royal Opera House tour: 9, 14 July.

Henry Wood prom. Wagner concert; Sladen, Nash, Llewellyn, cond. Sargent; *Boccanegra* and *Aida* excerpts, with Sladen, Coates, Matters, Glynn, cond. Sargent; 15 Sept.

Cavalleria Rusticana (Turiddu); Shuard, Alan, cond. Mudie; Sadler's Wells: 9, 20 Oct., 1, 14, 27 Nov., 8, 17, 26 Dec.

Turandot (new production) (Calaf); Gertrude Grob-Prandl, Blanche Turner, Dalberg, Kraus, Rhydderch Davies, Hannesson, Tree, cond. Barbirolli; Covent Garden: 22, 24 Oct., 12, 22 Nov.

Aida (concert version) (Radames); Amy Shuard, Janet Howe, Arthur Copley, Trevor Anthony, cond. Sargent: Kingston upon Hull: 7 Nov.

Messiah; Joan Alexander, Freda Townson, Stanley Clarkson, cond. Herbert Bardgett; Nottingham: 15, 17 Dec.

1952

Il Trovatore (Manrico); Brouwenstijn, Langdon, Walters, Watson, cond. Capuana; Covent Garden: 1, 5 Jan. With Drake, Price, Sharp, Clarkson, cond. Mudie,(revival); Sadler's Wells: 8, 12, 17, 23 Jan., 11, 23 Feb., 3, 13 March.

Cavalleria Rusticana (Turiddu); Shuard, Probyn, cond. Mudie; Sadler's Wells: 3, 21 Jan., 21 Feb.

Turandot (Calaf); Blanche Turner, Dalberg, R. Davies, Hannesson, Kraus, cond. Barbirolli; Covent Garden: 15 Jan., 10, 23 May. Royal Opera House tour: 25 Feb., 22, 29 Nov.

Madame Butterfly (Pinkerton); Shuard, Price, Dowling, cond. Mackerras; Sadler's Wells: 28 Jan., 16, 28 Feb., 12 March. With Sinclair, Sladen, Williams, cond. Capuana; Covent Garden: 31 May, 5, 9 June.

Aida (Radames); Zadek, Coates, Langdon, Raisbeck, Walters, cond. Barbirolli; Covent Garden: 1 Feb.With Brouwenstijn, Langdon, Nowakowski, Shacklock, Walters, cond. Barbirolli; 14, 17 April, 26, 28 June, 3, 6, 14 Nov. Royal Opera House tour: 27 Feb., 4, 10, 21, 24 March. Concert version with Shuard, Shacklock, Noble, Anthony, cond.Sargent; Royal Albert Hall: 22 March.

Concert, with Amy Shuard, excerpts from *The Mastersingers, Aida, Faust, Butterfly, Turandot, Il Trovatore;* Royal Albert Hall: 17 Feb.

Tosca (Cavaradossi); Royal Opera House tour: 1 March. Maria Kinasiewicz, Kraus, cond. Goodall; Covent Garden: 22, 29 April, 31 Oct.

Concert, Royal Festival Hall: 17 March.

Concert; Caxton Hall, Westminster: 10 April.

Bartered Bride (Jenik); Bower, Kentish, Glynne, cond. Gibson; Sadler's Wells: 13 May.

La Boheme (Rodolfo); Schwarzkopf, Walters, Glynne, Sladen, cond. Capuana; Covent Garden: 20 June.

Verdi's Requiem; Schwarzkopf, Eugenia Zareska, Norman Walker, cond. Victor de Sabata; Royal Festival Hall: 29 June.

Macbeth (Macduff); Rothmüller, Dalberg, Dorothy Dow, cond. Vittoria Gui; Glyndebourne: 2 July.

Henry Wood prom. Handel-Elgar; Marjorie Thomas, cond. Sargent; Royal Albert Hall: 17 Sept.

Faust (Faust); Gartside, Betty Sagon, Glynne, William Edwards; Dublin Gaiety: 1, 5, 6 Dec.

1953

La Boheme (Rodolfo); Veronica Dunne, G. Evans, Te Wiata, Walters, cond. Barbirolli; Covent Garden: 26 Jan.

Aida (Radames); Nowakowski, Sutherland, Brouwenstijn, Shacklock, Walters, cond. Barbirolli; Covent Garden: 28 Jan., 5, 11 Feb. Royal Opera House tours: 16, 23 Feb., 2, 18, 28 March, 1, 11, 15 April, 30 July, 1, 5, 10, 14, 19, 25, 29 Aug. With Raisbeck, Shacklock, Te Wiata, Geraint Evans, cond. Pritchard; Swansea: 17 Oct. With Brouwenstijn, Dalberg, Shacklock, Sutherland, Rothmüller, cond. Barbirolli/Young; Covent Garden: 2, 7, 11, 18, 26 Dec.

Il Trovatore (Manrico); Victoria Elliott, Angela Wheeldon, Stanley Clarkson, Jean Watson, cond. Mudie; Sadler's Wells: 3 Feb. Royal Opera House tour: 21, 28 Feb., 4, 16, 18 April. With Callas, Simionato, Walters, Langdon, cond. Erede; Covent Garden: 26, 29 June, 1 July. With Brouwenstijn, Rankin, Langdon, Walters, cond. Tausky; Covent Garden: 21, 25, 30 Nov., 5 Dec.

A Masked Ball (Riccardo); Sutherland, Walters, Coates, cond. Tausky; Royal Opera House tour: 11, 13, 16 March.

Turandot (Calaf); Grob-Prandl, Hannesson, R. Davies, Kraus, Turner, cond. Barbirolli; Covent Garden: 20, 28 April, 1 May.

Der Rosenkavalier (Tenor Singer); Sylvia Fisher, Glynne, Howitt, Leigh, Lewis, Shacklock, cond. Kleiber; Covent Garden: 29 April, 4, 9, 18, 29 May.

Carmen (new production) (Don José); Nell Rankin, Sutherland, Lewis, Frances Yeend, Langdon, Rothmüller, Donlevy, cond. Pritchard; Covent Garden: 2, 7, 10, 18, 26 Nov,. 28 Dec.

Hugh the Drover (Hugh); Pollak, Joan Stuart, Sharp, Owen Brannigan, Probyn, Dowling, cond. Dods; Sadler's Wells: 11, 13, 19 June.

Messiah; Jennifer Vyvyan, Nancy Thomas, Richard Standen, LSO, cond. Sargent; 14 Nov.

1954

Aida (Radames); Hammond, Sutherland, Shacklock, Rothmüller, cond. Young; Covent Garden: 22 Jan., 4 Feb. With Shuard, Hammond, Sutherland, Shacklock, cond. Young; Covent Garden: 3, 7, 11, 14 July. Revival, with Shuard, G. Evans, Glynne, Langdon, Shacklock, cond. Young; Covent Garden: 14, 20, 28 Dec. Royal Opera House tour: 24, 26 Feb., 10, 13 March, 3, 17 April.

Carmen (Don José); Shacklock, Sutherland, Rothmüller; 27 Jan., 9 Feb. With Shacklock, Geraint Evans, Langdon, Lanigan, Leigh, R. Lewis, Nilsson, Sutherland, cond. Pritchard/Downes; Covent Garden: 28, 30 Oct., 4, 6, 24 Nov. Royal Opera House tour: 8 March.

Il Trovatore (Manrico); Brouwenstijn, Langdon, Rothmüller, Watson, cond. Tausky; Covent Garden: 18 Feb., (broadcast), 20 Feb. With Victoria Elliott, Gita Denise, Dargavel, Sam Mooney; Dublin Gaiety: 11, 15 May.

Tosca (Cavaradossi); Royal Opera House tour: 6 March

Der Freischutz (revival) (Max); Royal Opera House tour: 16, 19, 23 March. With Sylvia Fisher, G. Evans, R. Davies, Kraus, Leigh, Walters, Langdon, cond. Downes; Covent Garden: 23, 27 April, 1, 13, 19 May, 11 June, 12, 16 July.

Madame Butterfly (Pinkerton); Rina Gigli, B. Sagon, B. Dargavel, cond. Tausky; Dublin Gaiety: 4, 6, 8 May.

The Beggar's Opera (Macheath); Lumsden, Iacopi, Marjorie Thomas, Kraus, Rose Hill, cond. del Mar; Sadler's Wells: 4, 9 Oct.

1955

Der Freischutz (Max); R. Davies, G. Evans, Kraus, Leigh, Nowakowski, Sutherland, cond. Downes; Covent Garden: 15 Jan.

Aida (Radames); G. Evans, Glynne, Langdon, Shacklock, Shuard, cond. Young; Covent Garden: 17, 21 Jan., 21 Feb., 23 April. With Sutherland, Shacklock, G. Evans, cond. Young; Royal Opera House tour: 1, 9, 12, 15, 29 March, 5, 9 April.

La Boheme (revival) (Rodolfo); Morison, G. Evans, Glynne, Hale, Robinson, Tree, Walters, cond. Goodall; Covent Garden: 9, 14, 16 Feb.

Carmen (Don José); Royal Opera House tour: 3, 31 March, 14 April. Revival with Marianna Radev/Una Hale, Sutherland, Langdon, Ronald Lewis, Ronald Firmager, cond. Downes/Hollingsworth; Covent Garden: 21, 29 June, 6 July, 20 Oct., 4, 14, 19, 24 Nov. With Shacklock, Carlyle, Sutherland, cond. Downes; Covent Garden: 27 Dec.

Bartered Bride (Jenik); Victoria Elliott, Gwent Lewis, cond. Dods; Sadler's Wells: Sept.

I Pagliacci (Canio); Patricia Bartlett, Hargreaves, G. Lewis, P. Glossop, cond. Gibson; Sadler's Wells: 23 May, 29 Sept.

Turandot (Calaf); Covent Garden: Grob-Prandl, R. Davies, Leigh, Dalberg, Walters, Lanigan, Nilsson, Tree, cond. Coodall. 15, 19, 21, 23 July. With Maria Kinas (formerly Kinasiewicz), Una Hale, Geraint Evans, Lanigan, Nilsson, cond. Goodall; Covent Garden: 26, 28 Oct., 9, 11 Nov.

Henry Wood prom., Jennifer Vyvyan, Norma Procter, Trevor Anthony, cond. Sargent; Beethoven, symphony No. 9; Royal Albert Hall: 16 Sept.

Madame Butterfly (revival) (Pinkerton); Shuard, Howitt, Tree, Walters, cond. Kempe; Covent Garden: 2, 8, 12, 18, 23 Nov.

Simone Boccanegra (revival) (Gabriele Adorno); Sharp, Glossop, Hargreaves, Glynne, Elliott, cond. Quayle; Sadler's Wells: 1, 13 Dec.

1956

Carmen (Don José); Shacklock, Hale, Veasey, Firmager, Langdon, cond. Downes; Covent Garden: 31 Jan., 4 Feb., 26, 29 June, 2 July. Royal Opera House tour: 28 Feb., 5, 10, 24 March, 4, 7 April.

Simone Boccanegra (Gabriele Adorno); Sadler's Wells: 11 Feb. With Victoria Elliott, Roderick Jones, Howell Glynne; Dublin Gaiety: 5, 7, 10, 12 Dec.

Sir John in Love (Fenton); R. Jones, Ronald Lewis, Heddle Nash, Owen Brannigan, Denis Dowling, Marion Lowe, cond. Stanford Robinson; BBC broadcast from Camden Theatre, London: 12 Feb.

Madame Butterfly (Pinkerton); Royal Opera House tour: 2, 8, 17, 21, 24 March, 10, 14 April. With Shuard, Howitt, Tree, Walters, cond. Kempe; Covent Garden: 28, 30 April, 16 May, 3, 19 July.

La Boheme (Rodolfo); Elsie Morison, Walters, Geraint Evans, Rhydderch Davies, Adele Leigh, cond. Kubelik; Covent Garden: 17 May.

Henry Wood prom; excerpts from *The Mastersingers;* Elizabeth Fretwell, Janet Howe, Karl Kamanan, Gwent Lewis, cond. Cameron; Royal Albert Hall: 9 Aug.

Tosca (Cavaradossi); Joan Hammond, Ronald Lewis; Dublin Gaiety: 26, 28 Nov., 1 Dec.

1957

Carmen (Don José); Muriel Smith/Resnik/Zareska, Sutherland, Allen, Langdon, Carlyle, Veasey, Firmager, Troy, cond. Matheson; Covent Garden: 5 Feb., 24, 27 May, 26 June. 15, 18 Nov. Royal Opera House tour: 16, 20, 27 March.

Turandot (revival) (Calaf); Sylvia Fisher, Shuard, Kelly, R. Lewis, Lanigan, Nilsson, Walters, cond. Kempe; Covent Garden: 4, 9, 13 May.

Il Trovatore (Manrico); Milanov, Rouleau, Howitt, Walters, Barbieri, Troy, cond. Downes; Covent Garden: 13 June.

Tales of Hoffman (revival) (Hoffman); Howitt, Dunne, Collier, Kraus, Tree, Troy, Lewis, Coertse, cond. Downes; Covent Garden: 9, 13, 16, 29 July. With Veasey, Sutherland, Langdon, Kraus, Studholme, Grant, cond. Downes; Covent Garden: 30 Oct., 5, 7, 13, 21 Nov. With Margaret Nisbitt, Joyce Barker, Veronica Dunne, B. Dargavel; Dublin Gaiety: 9, 14 Dec.

Concert; quintet, *Die Meistersinger*; Sutherland, Pease, Nilsson, Howe; broadcast from Royal Albert Hall: 11 Sept.

Concert; Ivy Sykes; Welwyn Garden City: 17 Nov.

1958

Aida (Radames); Brouwenstijn, Shacklock, Langdon, Troy, Carlyle, Walters, Robinson, cond. Emanuel Young; Covent Garden: 4 Jan., 14 June. Royal Opera House tour: 3, 8, 14, 17, 28 March.

Carmen (Don José); Shacklock, Allen, Hale, Langdon, Lewis, Firmager, Troy, cond. Matheson; Covent Garden: 4 Feb. With Resnik, Sutherland, Veasey, R. Lewis, cond. Matheson; Covent Garden: 24 June, 7, 14, 18 July. With Pollak, Bruce Boyce, Barbara Britton, cond. Havelock Nelson; Grand Opera House, Belfast: 29 April.

Centenary Gala; Covent Garden: 10 June.

Henry Wood prom; excerpts *Die Meistersinger;* Elizabeth Fretwell, Marjorie Thomas, James Pease, Dennis Stephenson, cond. Cameron; Royal Albert Hall: 20 Aug.

Tosca (Cavaradossi); Joan Hammond, Otakar Kraus; Dublin Gaiety: 25, 27, 29 Nov., 2 Dec. ☐

DISCOGRAPHY

COLUMBIA

1946

DB 2217 Woman is fickle *(Rigoletto)* - Jenik's aria *(Bartered Bride)*.

DX 1283-1301 *Messiah*.

1947

DX 1376 Love duet *(Madame Butterfly)* with Joyce Gartside.

DX 1408-23 *Elijah*.

DX 1455 Your tiny hand is frozen *(La Boheme)* - All hail thou dwelling (Faust).

1948

DX 1506 Oh horror! In pity hear me now *(Simone Boccanegra)* - *Prize song (The Mastersingers)*.

DX 1539 Ah yes! Thou'rt mine *(Il Trovatore)* - Flower song *(Carmen)*.

DX 1548 On with the motley *(Pagliacci)* - Turiddu's farewell *(Cavalleria Rusticana)* with Olwen Price.

1949

DB 2627 Star of the County Down - Ireland, Mother Ireland.

1950

DB 2745 Catari - Tis the day.

DX 1688 Song of the road *(Hugh the Drover)* - The English rose *(Merrie England)*.

1951

DX 1748 Santuzza/Turiddu duet *(Cavalleria Rusticana)* with Amy Shuard.

HMV

1948

B 9721 Bonny labouring boy - Dark eyed sailor.

C 3824 Forgive Amelia, trio *(Simone Boccanegra)* with Joyce Gartside and Howell Glynne.

C 3825 Weary and worn with suffering, finale Act 1 ensemble *(Simone Boccanegra)*.

ROYALE
1952
LP 1409 Glyndebourne *Macbeth*. James Johnston listed as "Horst Wilhelm".

BOOSEY & HAWKES
V 2102 My love's an arbutus.

UNPUBLISHED MATRIX
1946
CAX 10061 This one or that (Questa Quella)*(Rigoletto)*.
CAX 9488 Ev'ry lover's girl- I know a maiden *(Bartered Bride)* with Howell Glynne.

1951
CAX 10040 Celeste aida*(Aida)*.

TESTAMENT RECORDS
1994
SBT 1058 Commemorative compact disc containing a selection of the above recordings and the previously unissued material.

INDEX

In the 1951 Covent Garden production of **Turandot,** *Johnston as Calaf once struck the palace gong with such aplomb that it was dislodged from its fastenings and disappeared below stage. Calaf was his favourite role and his singing of Nessun dorma was always hugely popular with audiences.*

(Photograph by Barrett, courtesy of *Opera* magazine).

Redames in Aida *was one of the big roles in which Johnston was most at home.*